A BRIDGE TOO FAR
OR *SELDOM CROSSED*

The Value of Work Means Different Things
to Different People
Spanning Cultural Disparity in a Globalising
Labour Market

by
Ruby Welch

Strategic Book Publishing and Rights Co.

Strategic Book Publishing and Rights Co.
12620 FM 1960, Suite A4-507
Houston, TX 77065

www.sbpra.com

ISBN: 978-1-62857-555-2

Design: Dedicated Book Services, (www.netdbs.com)

TABLE OF CONTENTS

Introduction

This book draws on an investigation into work ethic that I conducted in 2007 for a PhD thesis in anthropology. This thesis argues that industrial relations are culturally shaped rather than solely determined by technological, industrial, or political considerations. Societies do change due to industrialization and technological innovation, but they do not necessarily converge because people in various social systems adapt to social change in culturally specific ways.

I gathered data by conducting interviews in the field and questionnaires on the internet, which led me to a detailed understanding of variations in attitude to the concept of work of culturally different people. I conducted my research in New Zealand during a period of significant change in the labour market, which allowed me to see that transformations in the job market do not necessarily coincide with changes in people's ideas about work. For instance, in the case of the Maori people in New Zealand, their ideational constructs of work continued to contrast greatly with those of mainstream New Zealanders. In the following chapters I take the phrase *ideational systems or constructs* to mean systems of thought that people carry in their heads, which direct their expectations and perceptions about work. These systems are composed of shared ideas, values, beliefs, rules, and meanings that are expressed through social institutions. Ideational systems also influence the ways in which people organize their workplaces, which are, in turn, subsystems of their broader society. Therefore, I argue that industrial relations are culturally shaped rather than solely determined by technological, industrial, or political events.

This book also distinguishes between individualistic ways of thinking about work in Western societies and the holistic and all-encompassing concepts of work among non-Western people. I present the Maori example of economic action and development to show that rather than conforming to the integrative efforts of consecutive New Zealand governments over the years, the Maori embarked on a course of self-determination shaped by their own cultural constructs. I also cite examples of other culture groups, such as minority groups in Japan and India and the Mormons in the United States. The latter group illustrates that even within Western cultures there are factions whose beliefs and values contrast mainstream ideals.

I have consulted many authors on the topic of the meaning of work, and their insights have been very helpful in the formulation of my thoughts. Their writings are cited at the end of this book. I owe a great deal of gratitude to those who participated in this study and gave me the information that I needed to understand the problems of the labour market. Special thanks go to my Maori participants, who patiently explained to me the issues they face in both the village and the city. Niek Veeken, a senior research specialist in the Netherlands, provided me with valuable insights into the labour market and the latest materials on policies and procedures. Last but not least, I would like to express gratitude to my supervisor, Dr. Helen Johnson, who helped me to focus on the relevant issues of my study in order to formulate my thoughts and express them in my work. Dr. Leon Satterthwait also provided the constructive advice to focus on the significance of my research, while Dr. Kathy Ahern explained how to organize my work and zoom in on the salient points. I am also grateful for the AMES Organisation in Auckland for enabling me to interview many of the workers who had been made redundant during the early 1990s by the restructuring forces in the labour market. They gave me insights into the importance of work in their lives and what it meant for them to be forced out of the workforce, which affected them not only economically, but also in their social standards and their families' standing in society.

Chapter 1
Work Ethic in the Searchlight

In this book I define work ethic as a culture's belief system associated with work. Based on research I carried out among the New Zealand Maori people, I argue that the concept of work means different things to different people. Although policy makers in Western societies presuppose that all actors in the labour market aspire to the same outcomes and rewards from their economic efforts, my research suggests this premise is false. I provide the principles that underlie my definitions of key concepts used, such as *work*, *work ethic*, and *the meaning of work*. I provide a description of the relevance of the study and its limitations and biases together with my position as researcher in the study.

In order to carry out an investigation of this nature, I first had to demonstrate its social worth. Why study the work ethic and meaning of work of indigenous and ethnic minority groups? Changes have taken place in the world of work as a result of the rise of information technology. This transformation of the labour market has created economic and social change on a global scale, leading to high levels of unemployment and the deregulation of working conditions in many developed nations. Previously, workers were integrated into a structure with socially established rights and duties. Almost all of life, including work, proceeded within the family circle, but as the nineteenth century progressed, work became increasingly separated from the family and the home, and a new cult of work sought to move it into the centre of human existence. Industrialization destroyed many old crafts as mechanization advanced, new technologies expanded, and machinery demanded more men to make, operate, and serve it.

The early nineteenth century saw an end of state control in Britain. No longer constrained to follow traditional wage practices, employers were able to test the market for required skills. As a result, workers learned to regard their labour as a commodity to be sold in a free capitalist economy although they were still inclined to fix their asking price by noneconomic criteria. This change illustrates the social aspect of the labour contract prior to the information revolution, when people were allowed to separate time spent at work from their time spent as ordinary citizens with home lives and family obligations. Employers were beginning to measure work by custom or precedent. A fair day's work was measured by social usage rather than crude market forces, and a less-than-market wage was considered acceptable in return for more independence, leisure, and respect.

The balance of work and home has undergone a fundamental change. Perhaps the key element in the industrial era that existed prior to the information age was the ability of the working class to organize into networks that represented their interests by bargaining collectively for rights, privileges, better conditions, and fair pay. During the first half of the nineteenth century, conflict between industrial workers and employers frequently resulted in workers leaving the workplace to form crowds in the streets to voice their objections. In 1799, the British government passed the Combination Act, which made meetings of organized workers' groups illegal and banned popular demonstrations. However, when it became apparent that the act tended to stimulate public disturbances rather than quell them, it was repealed. Soon trade unionism became a mass movement, and union activity became legalized in the last quarter of the nineteenth century. Unions developed to protect the material interests of workers in industrial settings in which they held little formal power.

My principal question in my research was how the Maori people of New Zealand and workers from other cultures perceive the concept of work. What sociocultural circumstances shape their perceptions, and what bearing do their perceptions have on behaviour patterns?

In asking how indigenous people perceive their economic activity, I also examined how broader socioeconomic changes have affected the systems of workers in the labour market. What bearing does the transformation of labour conditions and work environments have on the way people think about work? Are they all affected in the same way, irrespective of cultural background and position in the labour arena? How do indigenous people think about work, and what principles and motivations gave rise to these thoughts?

To ascertain people's thoughts about work, I considered the ideational, value, and belief systems of my study's participants in order to better understand what work means to people, how they govern economic activity, and what meaning work and normative values and beliefs have for those outside mainstream Western societies.

Although work patterns are generally considered the outcome of practical and economic decisions that are made in industrial arenas worldwide, my study shows they can equally be shaped by cultural aspects such as religious beliefs and family values, which, in turn, shape the norms that validate the purposes and ideologies of people's economic enterprise.

The key argument here is that *meaning* is a sociocultural process because people reveal their behaviour patterns and social and economic organization in their daily conversations. Roger Keesing, in his book *Anthropology, A Contemporary Perspective*, defines the process of creating meaning as "motives that guide choice, and the institutional framework within which choices take place." Hence, the meaning of work, if shaped within groups with a strong sense of ethnic identity such as the Maori of New Zealand, will reveal these salient principles of participation in economic activity and people's reasons for them as a distinctive work ethic. The problem is that changes in the world of work are supported by an economic ideology that the majority of the labour force has not yet caught up with, as sociocultural patterns change slowly and views about the right to work are ingrained in the minds of many workers.

Work is as old as humankind. However, employment only became a dominant form of social organization a mere two and a half centuries ago in Britain and in other parts of Europe. In the Western world the terms *work* and *employment* tend to be used interchangeably, which is not the case in many cultures that do not distinguish work from the rest of life. The Western term *employment* is associated with contractual work arrangements involving material rewards; it relates to paid work, and the contemporaneous use of both terms has become widely accepted in the West. Paid work is infused with moral and political values and ideas about social worth, so to lose one's job not only deprives one of income, but, equally, of status, identity, and rights, as abilities and motivation tend to be questioned. As a consequence work has taken a central place in our material existence, our position in the world, and every other aspect of life.

This positioning of work in the centre of life became a point of reference during my interviews with Maori participants, who held entirely different views on the subject. By teaching children to work from a young age, the Maori have a concept of work with wider connotations than merely working for wages. Maori ideas about work include taking care of the needs, interests, and welfare of all members of one's *hapu* (sub-tribe) and *whanau* (extended household). In subsequent studies, I found this view of work common in other non-Western societies.

The disturbing outcomes of modern market policies can be ascribed to the fact that developments in technology progress far more rapidly than ideas about work. Changes in the nature and organization of work have left the beliefs and values that workers associate with their jobs far behind, especially when the skills that they previously relied and prided themselves on are no longer marketable. This situation warrants inquiry into how being out of work affects all

workers and how Western researchers generally understand the idea of work.

Any study of the meaning and purpose of work must begin with the problem of how this widely used term has been defined. One author, Charles Handy, identifies the concept of work as "Western societies' chosen way of distributing income." Another, Paul Ransome, expands on this notion by pointing out that work can be defined as acts undertaken in the pursuit of the satisfaction of needs. Work reflects the basic human need for expression through action and is deliberately undertaken in pursuit of the satisfaction of recognized needs. Also, since all work is done either *with* other people or *for* others, it is essentially a social activity. Work, then, is an activity carried out for someone else in return for a wage designated by the person paying the wage and for a purpose not chosen by the worker. Work is often, therefore, identified with and limited to employment; employment is, undoubtedly, the dominant framework within which the production and distribution of goods and services takes place. In contrast, activities such as housework, looking after children at home, and voluntary work in the community are typically not considered work or employment because they do not engender income.

The concept of a work ethic also needs to be defined if it is to be used to determine how people think about work and how their perceptions guide their behaviour. In *The American Work Ethic and the Changing Work Force*, Herbert Applebaum argues that objects created by work reflect human culture, as humans take the materials of nature and use tools to fashion useful objects. The products of the mind and imagination also reflect human culture. Humans see, evaluate, and measure themselves by their work, as work enables them to construct a world that stands between themselves and nature. This view proposes that work ethic is essentially a human survival ethic, and that without work human society cannot exist. Humans need culture to create a system of values and behaviour, which are necessary for interaction with the human and natural worlds; therefore, work and culture are inseparable. Thus, a work ethic is a value system associated with carrying out work in a society with specific cultural patterns.

It is in this sense that I consider work ethic to be an *ideational system* created by the norms and values that result from people's views of their world and environment. Marshall Sahlins observed that *meaning* is a term that applies to cultural order, and that this meaningful system defines all functionality because no functional explanation is ever sufficient by itself, for functional value is always relative to the given cultural scheme. If work ethic, then, is an ideational system, an investigation into its varied meanings is incomplete if the values and beliefs of all workers are not afforded equal scrutiny. In this way, the varied meanings ascribed to the concept of work by people of different backgrounds and cultural heritage can be explored.

For this reason, one might argue that the groups most affected by drastic changes in the labour market might be the indigenous people and ethnic minorities in industrial areas of the West. The Maori people of New Zealand were brought into a Western cash economy when British colonizers arrived in their islands with their ideas of economic development and social organization. In this book, I use the experiences of some New Zealand Maori to illustrate the differences in ideational systems that include the concept of work, a work ethic, and the meaning of work, and to show how the concept of work means different things to different people. My Maori participants portray a dichotomy between the *Pakeha* (Western) concept of work and Maori beliefs and values about their economic activity. The latter diverge considerably from the work ethic of mainstream Pakeha society.

Relevance of the Study

In order to undertake a study of this kind, it must be relevant to existing conditions in the world of work. Thus, it is useful to acknowledge that there are differences and similarities among the world's people and that personal and social identities are anchored in the social order. People generally seek to improve their standing in the eyes of others in the community, and their personal worth is constantly judged by the community's standards and values.

An anthropologist of the 1960s, Ward Goodenough, labelled three types of culture: *private culture*, an individual's knowledge of beliefs, languages, and other people and the choices they make; *operating culture*, a person's guide to dealing with others; and *public culture*, the system of beliefs and norms shared among a society's members. A community's culture consists of the perpetual and conceptual features embedded in its language, belief systems, public symbols, values, rules, and operational procedures.

It is this area of culture in non-Western societies that values and beliefs about work have been adversely affected by changes in the labour market. Although dated, this idea of public culture is useful in describing the problems experienced by the workforce caused by disruptions in the world of work, the commonly accepted work ethic, and the habits of people at work. These changes have affected workers in mainstream Western societies but have especially affected indigenous people, who are more likely to be semi- or unskilled workers already disadvantaged by a lack of marketable skills and conflicting views on the standards and practices of their workplaces.

My investigation took place among the Maori workers in New Zealand, although they are represented in almost every occupation available in that country, they remain concentrated in unskilled and semiskilled jobs, overrepresented as labourers, drivers, and road workers. During the 1980s, Maori constituted 8.6 percent of the New Zealand population, compared to the Pakeha at 86 percent, yet they made up 64 percent of those employed in factory production and labouring work. There is no reason to believe that the situation has improved since the mass redundancies of the 1990s, when large sectors of unskilled and semiskilled workers were retrenched.

The Maori are not incapable of reaching professional heights in the market. But through my interviews with Maori participants, I found that they value opportunities for individual advancement less than opportunities to be part of a group on the job and to contribute to kin and community causes. Sadly, their position in the labour market can also be attributed to Maori youth leaving school too early, wasting talents and skills and finding little opportunity or encouragement to improve their chances in the labour force. Moreover, the Pakeha ideology of equality of opportunity blames the Maori nonachiever for lack of ambition and contends that if he or she fails, it is his or her own fault, because the world does not owe the Maoris a living and they have been given every chance. Such a position does not take into account that different cultures have different ways of judging what is relevant to their quality of life and choosing what they want to gain through work.

The three types of culture discussed earlier are useful for assessing the Maori people's position within Pakeha society and their consequent behaviour and attitudes. Beliefs are shared by members of a society, and when they are acted upon, they produce behaviour that is intelligible to other members of that society. Cultures are learned through language, and people maintain cultures to deal with problems or matters that concern them; a culture must strike a balance between the self-interest of individuals and the needs of society as a whole. It is for this reason that anthropology has turned its attention to the problems of everyday life in our own societies rather than focus its efforts on remote cultures.

Globalisation has become the academic and media buzzword of the early twenty-first century. The present phase of globalisation embodies a convergence of separate but interrelated factors, such as post-Fordism, innovations in technology, and neoliberal economic ideology. The Fordist understanding of work is based on the regulation of working time, realms of work, and industrial relations. In contrast, post-Fordist society demands flexible working conditions, which lead to a wide variety of employment situations and work experiences. The true importance of globalisation is that it provides an alternative way of understanding and opens the field to previously ignored subjects. My study shows that as the global labour market continues to transform, local people interpret globalising phenomena in their own culture-specific ways.

If anthropological theory needs to describe and understand the developments that have taken place in societies around the globe, it must also be able to analyse their impact on populations and, most significantly, the ways that local people are interpreting and interacting with global sociocultural change. I studied how workers cope with changes in the modern labour market and what effect the changes may have on their work ethic, or their beliefs and values about work. I explored how the Maori people in New Zealand and workers from other ethnic backgrounds experienced such changes.

There are two broad definitions of development. The first is referred to in the social sciences as *industrialization and modern communication*; it suggests progress in many industrial and social areas. The second takes into account how development tends to destroy indigenous cultures, disrupt communities, and marginalize individuals in the process of modernization. I have observed that changes in the labour market have indeed disrupted the lives of workers who experienced standardized labour regulations and predictable working conditions in the Fordist era. The tendency to marginalize sections of the workforce through mass redundancies poses a real threat to workers, especially to those who do not possess the skills to compete effectively in the labour market.

This book is also concerned with the question of whether changes in the labour market have equally affected Maori people and workers in mainstream society, or whether differences in work ethic may have allowed the Maori to view their options in other terms and to work towards different outcomes. The findings of this book are relevant because globalisation forces social change on local communities, indigenous people, and on most individuals in the labour market. Reactions to social change are not universal; they vary because of cultural and environmental differences and the way by which communities and the nations of the world have organized their economic and social systems. We are therefore compelled to recognize that people and the world they live in are just a bit more complex than we have previously thought.

A study of the effect of labour market reform on people's ideational systems, particularly in relation to work, is appropriate in the light of ongoing labour market changes, such as the Industrial Relations Reforms Act, which incensed workers (as reported frequently in the media) when it came to effect in June 2006 in Australia. In New Zealand in the early 1990s, the Individual Employment Contract Act was passed. Through my involvement with some workers' coalitions and movements, I learned that this act gravely limited the powers of the trade unions in New Zealand and marginalized individuals whose bargaining positions were threatened in a market that demanded new skills. Maori workers' job security also came under threat, as they were compelled to sign individual contracts and work in environments with co-workers who were non-Maori, rather than working in Maori groupings as in the past. As the participants explain in later chapters, Maori are reluctant to face Pakeha bosses in one-to-one job interviews, especially if the interviewer happens to be female. Some of the male Maori participants ascribed this to issues surrounding a man's *mana* and explained that dealings with women in a Maori environment are strictly governed by rules of *tapu*.

If developments in the world of work are found to have caused ideational systems about work to become secularized and at odds with religious roots and accepted norms, it would be necessary to investigate whether similar trends are found in beliefs about work among other indigenous people and ethnic minorities in society. Might these changes have resulted in the same disturbing consequences for these groups, or might they have resulted in different outcomes? Could it be that other factors may have circumvented the onslaught of market forces upon their work experiences, or might their working conditions have deteriorated even further?

It is clear that the transformation of the global labour market over the last two decades has rendered work ethic itself problematic for post-industrial society, as the market no longer guarantees suitable and permanent work for the workforce. New work practices, which need to keep pace with technology, are slow to emerge, causing fissure between people's expectations about their employment and the reality of the workplace. Furthermore, elements of uncertainty in today's job market cause employees to become suspicious of employers, as relations between them have suffered. My research may provide helpful insights into problems of employer–employee relations and facilitate more informed policy making. It may prove to be useful for contemporary theory about the issues and conditions generated by the concept of work. Globalisation is here to stay, but isn't it time that we seek the globalisation that we want and need?

Ethical Concerns

My personal involvement in the labour market situation during the 1990s and frequent association with Maori people in New Zealand have provided a context for this book and insights into the practices of the groups involved. I also consulted various authors' works about the labour market and Maori culture to anchor my research on changes in the modern labour market, my investigation of the Maori work ethic, and the impact of labour market changes on both Maori and Pakeha participants. Asking for personal information about people's experiences in the job market posed challenges. If employed, the information given by the participant could expose them and jeopardize their job situation. If unemployed, certain statements about financial options could imperil a participant's eligibility for social security assistance. As I did not ask for details that would identify my participants, my ethical considerations were more concerned with the information that Maori participants provided about the solutions they had found to being out of work in the cities and the explanations they gave for being "streetwise." Such information tended to place my participants in direct conflict with the rules and regulations in place for those who receive unemployment benefits.

Nonetheless, my Maori participants appeared not to be concerned about this possible consequence to the interview. In contrast, they were initially reluctant to pass on information about cultural issues, which could have tribal repercussions rather than negative Pakeha-related results. Thus, they provided this information in somewhat guarded terms. They asked, "Why do you want to know about how I feel as a Maori about my work?" The participants only glanced at the questionnaires, preferring instead to talk into the tape recorder. It was not until they perceived my knowledge of Maori culture and history that we came together to talk about Maori issues as friends rather than opposites. Yet my efforts to meet with prospective participants often ran into noncooperation from various Maori organizations. Fortunately, a helping hand came from the minister of Maori affairs after instructions from then-Prime Minister Helen Clark, who was aware of my inquiries into the world of work during the 1990s. I was recommended to conduct my research at Waipareira Trust Village in Henderson, Auckland.

In order to protect the participants and their information, I addressed them with aliases that could not possibly identify them. In this environment, my participants felt free and willing to offer their contributions to the research and to speak about cultural issues.

Chapter 2
Work Ethic and the World of Work

Many people in Western societies regard work as the most important aspect of their lives and consider the right to work of concomitant significance. Furthermore, most social interactions are shaped by values and beliefs that are constituted within ideational systems. In Western societies, values and beliefs regarding work are encompassed by the concept of work ethic, yet what may be categorized as work ethic differs in form and arrangement across cultures. This chapter provides a review of the history of work ethic and the ways in which work is perceived differently across and within cultures. It shows how culture shapes the way people think about their social institutions and how their ways of thinking form their attitudes toward and expectations of the organizations in their societies. A fitting discussion about work in Western societies should start with the description of the origins and history of the Protestant work ethic and proceed with a discussion about industrial relations in the contemporary world of work.

First we must ask which activities are generally accepted as work in Western societies. We may accept that the economy consists of two realms: the community and the market. Both facets constitute the economy, because humans are motivated by social fulfilment as well as instrumental purpose, competition, and the accumulation of gains. In this sense, community can be defined as real, on-the-ground associations and solidarities that people experience, in contrast to the market, which is composed of anonymous and short-term exchanges. Authors' theories about the workplace suggest that we must focus on the implications of human economic action and its expected function of integrating its organization—such as the division of labour, the relations in the workplace, and the belief systems that underlie the meaning that people attach to their daily toil—into the wider social system.

There is a range of ways to conceptualize work in Western societies. For example, all human beings carry out tasks that involve the use of mental and physical effort in order to produce goods and services that cater for any other type of action. The desire to work is a powerful need, a drive to self-expression, power, and creativity. However, workers' aspirations are valid only in terms of their own experience and needs. Such productive activity tends to occupy a larger part of their lives than a range of other definitions of reality. People carry mental programs in their heads, which are expressed in the values that compose their belief systems.

Thus, we are able to distinguish between two types of work. First, the previous era's industrial concept of work, which created a rather homogeneous experience for most workers through standardized rules promoting stability in the workplace. Second, the modern labour market, which is characterized by contractual regulations and more flexible organizational structures. Many are predisposed to define work as purely economic in essence, as opposed to the view that work consists of economic and cultural flows. Ideational factors shape the way people think about their social institutions; therefore, belief systems associated with the concept of work in any given society are also a product of culture.

To apply this notion to the belief and value constructs of the New Zealand Maori, it is necessary to consider that the dominant mode of production prior to European contact with indigenous people was kin-ordered, with the lineage or tribe determining division of labour and what should be produced. Keith Sinclair, a historian in the 1980s, described traditional Maori life as consisting of an extended kinship organization made up of *hapu* (sub-tribes) and *whanau* (extended family groupings). Maori belonging to these groups were members of a community in a sense that their individualistic European counterparts were not. Life for Maori people was, and in many aspects still is, a communal experience, as most activities were shared and performed for the sake of the community. The concept of private property was virtually unknown to the Maori people, and the mercantilist mode of production was imposed on them by Europeans during colonization

The transformation from kin-ordered to capitalist production affected nearly every aspect of Maori life, breaking up lineages and undermining leadership. Belief systems guide people's aspirations and hopes for the future when they engage in economic activity. Formal employment in Western counties endorses the wider social participation or citizenship of the individual, provides a means for participation in society, and is associated with feelings of community and self-worth. As work became central to society, its emphasis partly shifted from productive effort to social standing, and therefore the loss of a job deprives a person of a place of work, the company of workmates, and a source of income. Formal employment gives the individual public legitimacy and status based on principles of use, values, and a sense of worth.

While the notion of work is as old as humankind, reliance on it as a means to secure a way of life dates only from the late eighteenth and the beginning of the nineteenth century. Since then, employment, or paid work, has generally involved material rewards. The terms *work* and *employment* are deeply imbedded in our habits of speech but are often interchangeably used, which does present a problem when the concepts of culture and worldview are applied to the study of work. Work is essential for both individuals and societies, but for its performance the work values of those who engage in productive activity, or their expectation of it, bears most significance. Status, values, education, training, and occupation characteristics all shape the framework for work practices in a given environment.

Work ethic has become a principle that advocates that *work is good in itself*; one becomes a better person by virtue

of its practice. In other words, the work ethic to which Westerners commonly adhere stresses work as one's duty to society. Work is perceived as a crucial part of the social contract
in return for which society provides certain rights and protection for its citizens. Cultural differences in beliefs about
work are likely to create different ideas about, and rules for,
participation in the workforce, thereby complicating Western definitions of work ethic. Human thought is ultimately
social in its origins, functions, forms, and applications, and
it permeates all spheres, such as the home, marketplace, and
public arena. It is therefore clear that beliefs associated with
work must also be considered products of culture. However,
while associations and imagined solidarities in places of
work are considered important for workers, market forces
tend to be anonymous and impervious to people's expectations. Consequently, work ethic becomes problematic for
many sectors of the workforce, as current market policies
seem to be directly opposed to the norms and values that
support it.

The conditions of the labour market in the information
age, with the redundancy of semi- and unskilled workers
and the prominence awarded to knowledgeable and skilled
personnel, negate the working people's accepted rules of
society, which stipulate that citizens in jobs support their
community and those who do not work are a burden to the
general public. New information and communication technologies have transformed the industrial relations system
and workplaces in such a way that even workers who felt
secure in their jobs and expected to retain them until they retired have been made to feel that their employment could be
terminated at any time. Many of my participants commented
on how they have come to feel disenfranchised in the world
of work as their rights to work and contributions in society
are steadily taken away from them. Indeed, unemployment
is unwelcome because of the special role and meaning work
has in industrial society and the feeling that one's worth is
measured by the status of one's employment.

During the industrial period, economies rose and fell as the demands for goods and services increased and decreased. As a result, the job market fluctuated and any recession in the money market put many workers out of their jobs. With the next rise in the economy, however, the market invariably bounced back with a renewed demand for goods, services, and skilled workers, which indicates that innovation and profit are the driving forces of capitalist growth. Stephen Gudemand identified Henry Ford's innovation of the conveyor belt as a form of production that changed the relationship between tools and humans, how humans use the environment and the objects produced, and human relations in production.

The Fordist industrial relations system after World War II was the crowning glory of modern social reform, as work became a means of socialization. Now regulated by law, working conditions were no longer determined exclusively by commercial considerations. A functional, non-disruptive model based on collective action developed, and was relatively successful at regulating conflict. The social aspect of the concept of work became stabilized due to the creation of large-scale social organizations and the institutionalization of the social aims and responsibilities of both public- and private-sector companies in relation to the workforce. This organizational society was based on the principle of creating large producers of goods and services subject to bureaucratic regulation to achieve a balance between public and private, under the assumption that a degree of state control of the market was necessary to achieve social goals. It also recognized the necessity for companies to build these social goals into their own structures to ensure social accounting, worker participation, and social democracy in places of work.

The developments in the world of work over the last two decades in many Western societies have rendered this social contract between the work sphere and society problematic for most sectors of the workforce. Market rules were rewritten as the industry shifted from standard Fordism to post-Fordist regulations, undergoing radical restructuring and moving the basis of production to international localities. Though globalisation may be conceived by some as theory or ideology, reality indicates that much of traditional production has been transferred to semi-peripheral parts of the world economy while automation has largely caused the disappearance of the mechanical tasks that formed a standard part of the Fordist era. Production was made more flexible in an effort to accommodate markets that had become unpredictable as a result of fierce international competition and technological innovation. In other words, it wasn't job availability that was suspended but *workers' skills*. These were permanently wiped off the job slate by modern technology, as one person aided by machines can do the work of many.

The concept of companies' social responsibility has undergone an equally major transformation in the transition from regulatory models of working patterns to flexible production methods that have a fundamental impact on the essence of citizenship at the interface between labour rights and general political rights. New information and communication technologies have transformed the industrial relations system and its workplaces in such a way that even those workers who felt secure in their jobs and expected to retain them until they retired, realized soon that their employment could terminate at any time. Workers have come to feel vulnerable in the world of work as their rights to work and participation in society as contributing citizens are steadily eroded. In order to grasp the meaning of the impact of social changes in today's market, it is important to examine historical developments in work over the last few centuries.

The History of Work in Western Societies

Humans have always been engaged in productive activity. Reliance on it as a means to secure a way of life, however, dates only from the late eighteenth and the beginning of the nineteenth centuries, when the early stages of industrialization transformed the economic and social structures of Great Britain and, sometime later, other parts of Europe. Work did not appear to be of central interest to the working class at this time, as it was regarded as a means to an end and not necessarily as an end in itself.

Initially, the notion that work is good was associated with the rise of Calvinism, or Puritan thought; it provided a favourable setting for labour to rise to prominence. Ideas about the benefits of work can be traced back to the Calvinist system of beliefs, which anchored work ethic in the religious teachings of John Calvin, who proclaimed that man could only achieve salvation in the afterlife with hard work and that idleness was to be regarded as sin. Indeed, it was not until the Reformation that physical labour became acceptable for all sections of the community, the wealthy included, and became part of an economic structure that was considered to be ordered by God. Work in all its forms came to mean more than putting food on the table, as it was now infused with moral and political values and ideas about social worth. To consider only technological changes in the labour market would render my research incomplete; the economic and social motivation of workers and the guidelines by which they are informed must be considered as well.

Studies of the autobiographies of working people from the 1820s to the 1920s reveal that in the early stages of industrialization, work was regarded as a means of survival, whereas workers' values and beliefs were primarily framed by religious views that formed the basis for their expectation of life outside the workplace. As the nineteenth century progressed, places of work moved from the home to the factory floor, where a "new cult of work strove for a place in the centre of human existence" (Burnett 1974). This development can be described by how the importance attached to labour first demonstrated itself in the distinction between productive and unproductive labour, later in the differentiation between skilled and unskilled work, and, finally, in the division of all activities into manual and intellectual labour.

Contemporary working time and experience have broken with the earlier model of standardized time, and it is very tempting to associate this development with the introduction of new technologies in the production process and with what is now commonly called "the new economy," but these changes need to be viewed as the spread of a new model of production to the economy as a whole.

At this point, a distinction needs to be made between the developments of mercantilism—the growth of commercial facts, guilds, urbanization, and a commercial class—and the rise of capitalism as an economic system of private ownership of property and a means of production and distribution that is based on profit and takes place within a free, competitive market in which supply and demand determine price. Mercantilism and capitalism were never clearly demarcated; the former simply merged into the latter over a few hundred years. Most significantly, wage labour was transformed into a commodity to be bought and sold, a development that clearly defined it as a characteristic of capitalism. Wherever capitalism became the dominant socioeconomic form for indigenous people, transformations and disruption of culture, social structure, economic modes of production, and political systems were inevitable. Indigenous people's property was privatized by Europeans either by theft or legal manipulation. My research suggests that this occurred with large sectors of rural Maori people who were deprived of most of their lands—either through confiscation or illegal purchase—and forced to migrate to urban centres to work for low wages in the freezing works, on the roads, and wherever there was need for cheap labour.

The Protestant Work Ethic

Two distinct streams of thought dominated the Protestant work ethic. The first was that of Karl Marx, who stated that beliefs about work grew out of changes in the economic foundations of society and the need for new values to support the new ways of behaviour. The second perspective was advanced by Max Weber, who maintained that Calvinism had developed a set of beliefs that focused on the concept of predestination, which encouraged its followers to pursue occupations that yielded unlimited profits and taught that wealth was a sign that one was among God's elect. The Protestant ethic, therefore, provided religious sanctions for the limitless accumulation and reinvestment of capital through diligent hard work, while at the same time prescribed austere living. The early capitalists were scarcely aware that they had initiated significant change in society, when through their desire and motivation to rank among the elect of God, economic success became the main symbol of their achievements. This work ethic, which morally justified profit making through hard work, spread throughout Europe and America, but over time its religious aspects began to fade; only the expectation of due reward for hard work became interwoven with the norms of Western culture.

The religious concept of work as recompense for sin gave rise to the view that being out of work was sinful. These beliefs became embedded in the economic realities of the poor and contributed to the advancement of the Protestant ethic. Yet it is at odds with developments in the world of work, as large sectors of workforces in Western societies have been made redundant and having a job is no longer based on willingness to work but the quality of one's skills. These developments undermine normative beliefs about the right to work and diminish people's self-respect. Furthermore, the materialistic aspect of the work ethic, which promises psychological as well as monetary rewards for work, destroys the sense of purpose and fulfilment of people who work on assembly lines as well as those whose chances in the labour market have become more limited.

The promise of economic rewards for work also came under threat from the new factory system, as industrial plants began to produce more than the nation could use and hard work and production failed to provide a guaranteed share in prosperity. The profound economic and political changes stimulated by the rise of technology and science in the twentieth century saw the emergence of a social and cultural movement that would dominate Western thought in the new age of rationality and enlightenment. As the people of the mid-nineteenth century encountered tremendous cultural and social change with the ushering in of the industrial age, the people of the late twentieth century experienced equally substantial economic and social shifts at the start of the information age.

The steam engine augmented the transformation of European economic life, and capitalism reached across the world to include other cultures and societies. Industrial capitalism soon replaced mercantile capitalism and brought about radical change in the meaning of knowledge as it came to be applied to tools and production processes. The invention of the microchip in the late twentieth century accelerated this process as advanced knowledge was applied to machinery and tools to an unprecedented extent, affecting people's lives, work environments, and social structures, often with adverse outcomes for workforces in many Western societies.

Globalisation is an ongoing process with a long history, and it needs to include in its terminology the word *contemporary* to indicate the latest phase in its development. The ideology of economic neoliberalism has been added to its premise in order to promote the idea that economic integration will ensure great cooperation among people and countries and lead to world peace. However, many authors contend that the contemporary globalising market is producing disastrous outcomes for many members of the workforce, as their skills have been rendered useless in the modern market and a large proportion of workers have been marginalized into casual or temporary jobs. Neoliberalism favours the rich, and neoliberal adjustments invariably undercut domestic production prices, cause unemployment, create sweatshops, disrupt families, and encourage environmental despoliation. Neoliberalism has also resulted in increased outsourcing of jobs to destinations outside the workplace and even outside the country.

Adverse outcomes for workers suggest that in-depth studies of industrial relations are needed in order to analyse the trends in a globalising market and the effects they have on participants. Technological developments have escalated beyond the point where people can match them with their ideas about work. Hence, it is not only the Protestant ethic that is under threat, but every system of belief about work as well. Changes in the world of work have conveyed mixed messages about work ethic as relations between workers and their employers have radically shifted. Loyalty between employers and employees has suffered and, according to many participants, effectively disappeared. In modern industrial societies, social cohesion is mainly expressed through work and extended into social citizenship, that is, the interaction between work and citizenship is connected to the web of social ties that hold a society together. However, in order for societies to cohere, work needs to be stable and predictable for most people. The changes that have taken place over the last two decades in the labour market have shown that the new ways of structuring work, time, space, and employment contracts work together to undermine the social contract between workers and their societies.

As work is the main source of financial security in most people's lives, instability in work has a direct impact on the stability of personal life, a concern expressed by most of my participants. The relationship between the way things are and the way things ought to be is complex, as the relationship may be viewed in terms of identification, whereby what is normal is considered acceptable. People may experience a sense of powerlessness when their expectations of normality are no longer addressed. My participants expressed this concern, demonstrating indecision and bewilderment about their options in the workforce. Their concern suggests that if changes have occurred in what people have traditionally expected of their participation in work and society, and if that expectation is now undermined by an ideology in the labour market that has left workers unsure of their future prospects in the world of work, this might have consequences on what is generally accepted as ethic.

Business discussions on radio and television stations in both Australia and New Zealand invariably refer to corporate or business ethics rather than work ethic. Such terminology suggests that the social expectations that supported work ethic in the past have now switched from the social to the commercial arena. Thus, recent technological innovations have shaped global business practices and people's beliefs and expectations about work.

The technological innovation that has had the greatest effect upon people was the invention of the printing press in the mid-fifteenth century. The printed work promoted a rebirth of learning, education became more available to most, and Europe's lead in knowledge and technological innovation was established. Industrial capitalism soon replaced mercantile capitalism as knowledge was applied to tools, processes, and products. Technology became increasingly applied to work in the post-WWII period, and the invention of the microchip in the late twentieth century accelerated change in the market as advanced knowledge was aimed at machinery and tools to an unprecedented extent, changing people's lives, workplaces, and societies.

Capitalism and technical advance could not possibly have made such an impact worldwide without a radical change in the meaning of knowledge, which rendered the dominance of modern capitalism inevitable. The new information- and knowledge-based technologies contributed to a model of work in which knowledge is the key element. A second factor is the role of human capital—the new ideas, new solutions, and creativity that constitute a central element in the production process—while a third factor concerns the organization of labour to ensure the satisfactory functioning of this model of work.

The Factor of Human Capital

In industrial society, valuable resources and the means of production remain in the hands of those who own them; in a post-industrial labour market, valuable knowledge and skills are owned by individuals who take their expertise with them. Company managers are well aware of this development in the labour market, and although certain workers are easily dispensed with, valuable skills have a high price in a fiercely competitive market.

As the loyalty of employers toward workers significantly waned during the large-scale retrenchments of the 1990s, employers became painfully aware that employees had developed a predisposition to leave their jobs for better opportunities elsewhere. The decline of the employment relationship, and the model of social dialogue between the parties in the workforce, can be ascribed to the transformation of stable employment into temporary agency work, imposed part-time work, self-employment, and undeclared employment. The market can only be as good as its actors, because it depends on human capital as a vital resource for its survival. If this resource becomes a scarce commodity, economies cannot survive in an intensely aggressive global market. Policy makers need to understand these new trends and adjust their policy making to increase productivity rather than undermine workers' rights and ability to fully participate in their places of work.

Irrespective of trends in the labour market and the incentives of employers to limit staff numbers, work motivation appears to be weakening in the face of a lack of fair reward for hours spent on the job. The failure to appreciate the value of employees' input threatens any employing firm with the risk of losing its best people to higher bidders in the skills market. Other than recognition for a job well done in the form of fair pay, employees want to be valued for their performance and treated as assets rather than dispensable commodities. A key way to motivate employees to identify with the company and contribute to its success is to recognize and reward effort in order to generate workers' dependability. Conversely, people want employers to pay them above market rates; they insist that the key to creating a work environment that encourages motivation on the part of the workers lies in the wants and needs of individuals.

Work offers security, and insecurity at work causes suffering. Work has a direct impact on personal dignity and well-being because work is central to people's lives, and instability at work translates into personal insecurity. We cannot form a clear idea of what constitutes work ethic and how market conditions affect workers without people's own versions of their work experiences. In understanding different ideas about work, work ethic, and people's work experiences, it's necessary to understand culturally different ideas about work.

Perspectives of Work across Cultures

Anthropological research across cultures uncovers different ideas about work. Anthropology is based on the fact that humans make choices, and that their choices do not simply depend on material payoffs, but also on values and symbolic meanings. To set aside the symbolic motives and values around which people organize their lives and to argue that the motive to work is directed by pure ecological reason distorts the human motive to engage in economic activity.

The authors Katy Gardner and David Gil agree that people's basic needs are culturally determined and that although human work has biological roots, it is socially defined and shaped. They argue that work in the context of a society affects the experiences and development of workers and the social and cultural environments of the community, while the society shapes the work context and the workers. Hence, workers make meaning within a constantly changing social arena. At this point it is necessary to clarify the concept of meaning and how people construct meaning within different cultures.

Meaning, according to Eduardo Crespo, is a social process linked with personal identity and the ideas that people express in their daily conversations. This premise is helpful for developing the idea that work and life expectations are voiced through cultural experience. Therefore, I have treated the concept of meaning as something that is intended to be conveyed, or an action intended to be carried out in a certain way. Meaning can be explained as humans making sense of the world, a process in which knowledge is at once maintained and transformed, a process that makes each of us what we are and provides us with our ideas about the world. This explanation enables me to use the concept of meaning as a social process by which ideas and experiences can be interpreted and clarified.

Perception affects what humans perceive and how they understand what they perceive. Thus, humans not only engage in activities but also shape their actions according to their lived experience. Such lived experiences differ according to the cultural context in which they occur. In this sense I consider work ethic to be an ideational system, in terms of being a body of ideas and norms that vary across cultures.

Therefore, anthropologists ought to be able to explain the latest trends in the world of work and how they affect the workforce by studying the social factors that underpin people's beliefs about their participation in the labour market and the way they articulate these beliefs. Such an investigation would need to analyse how the ideational system of the right to work has developed over time and the way in which it is now threatened. The ideational system points to inconsistency between the reality and expectations of work, as there no longer appears to be a link between the reality of work life and reasonable expectations for work life for a large number of workers.

While the information age has benefited certain sectors in society, for others it has come with a social and material cost in quality of life and future prospects. Indeed, the notion of work in post-industrial times is rather ironic, since enforced idleness, through mass redundancies or loss of job, seems to be the price many are paying for improved efficiency. Some workers have work and money but often too little time, whereas others have time but no work or money because they have to rely on casual, impermanent job options.

The notion that meaning is a process suggests that work ethic is an expression of concepts and a system of symbols that vary between societies. Human beings not only engage in activities but also shape their actions and activities, which in turn are received by the consciousness given by inner experience. Thus, differences in culture can be seen as differences in experience, or, in other words, variations of feelings and expectations. People of different cultures may be subjected to the same conditions, environments, and practices in their places of work, but differences in the expression of lived experiences can vary, as they contain socially constructed units of meaning. Consequently, the problem is contained in the relationship between experience and expression.

As culture represents an ordered system of meaning and symbols in terms of which social interaction takes place, it forms the framework for beliefs, expressive symbols, and values by which individuals define their world, express feelings, and make judgments. In this context, culture is the vehicle through which human beings give meaning to their experiences and guide their actions. For example, religion formulates ideas about the overall shape of reality, but it also contains symbolic resources for expressing emotions, moods, sentiments, passions, and opinions. Religious perspectives enable humans to perceive and encapsulate aspects of their environment and pass on their way of seeing as knowledge from generation to generation.

Over time, religious ways of thinking about work have faded from Western socioeconomic practices and have been replaced by materialistic characteristics. However, Maori participants insisted that religious observance still features prominently in Maori socioeconomic practices, although some of their traditions have faded as a result of their absorption into mainstream New Zealand society.

If we accept social structure as a network of social relations and the form that action takes, we may ask what constitutes the general nature of the actor's life and what gives rise to it. A plausible answer may be found in the facts of everyday life and their associated implications for a work ethic. People's views contain essential aspects of a given culture; they are characterized by a standard explanation of the meaning of life and the universe and a set of facts. Thus, we may assume that a work ethic is strengthened and sustained by a distinct view of the world, which may be further influenced by religious beliefs. The characteristic in which human action is to be considered, from either a moral or aesthetic point of view, depends on the emotional life of the individual who experiences it. How an individual manages emotional economy becomes his or her primary concern in terms of what else is ultimately reasoned. As Marshall Sahlins, an anthropologist of the 1970s, so beautifully put into words: "There is connection between religion and practice when the mere cutting of logs evokes a special relationship between man, tree, and deity."

The study of globalisation breaks significantly from the traditional practice of anthropology, in which participant observation focused on local, bounded communities that could be studied in some depth over a year or two. The study of globalisation will not absorb the rest of anthropology, but will offer an alternative way of understanding subjects that have been ignored in the past. In this sense, globalisation can be understood as the reshaping of local conditions by powerful global forces on an ever-intensifying scale, suggesting an interconnectedness of cultural interaction and change. Studies of globalisation must, therefore, show how its forces exist in the context of different ways of being in Western and non-Western societies. Although people may continue to live local lives, increasingly they have become part of the globalising economy. In the context of globalisation, multicultural societies that embrace people from a variety of backgrounds must address issues of differing rights, different cultural understandings of what it means to be human, and the rights to which all humans are entitled.

Economic Practices in the Context of Market, Community, and Values

As stated earlier, economic practices and relationships are contained within the two realms of market and community. They are based on social relationships, trade and accumulation, importance that varies across societies, and economic practices that are always placed within a value context. The realms of community and market are largely considered separately in contemporary discussions on the economy because neoclassical economics primarily focuses on one value domain: the market. It is seen as a separate sphere comprising the whole of the economy, in which all goods are priced and rendered available for exchange.

A second point to be considered is the Western understanding of value, often viewed in contemporary economic theories as the outcome of individual preference based on demand and supply, which determines the price and value of goods. Value is locally specified, culture is made and remade through contingent categories such as home and work, and an economy is made up of different value arenas. This view casts light on the Maori perspective of economy because it exposes the fundamental value systems on which Maori beliefs about work are based, how they relate to their social institutions, and how their existence is symbolically

constituted—in other words, how they are culturally ordered.

Work is understood and explained in different ways by
Maori people. A distinct division of labour exists in "Maoridom," an expression used by Maori people. This division is
based on men being *tapu*, sacred or ritually restricted, and
women being *noa*, common or unrestricted. The distinction
between the domestic and public spheres did not become
important considerations for the Maori until after they began
migrating to urban centres. The distinction tends not to exist
so much between home and work spheres, but rather in the
separation between things Pakeha—mainstream society—
and things Maori.

It is culture, not resources, that determines how people
can make a living and what tools they need to convert material things into useful products. This process of making a
living can be referred to as *economic activity*. Different societies use diverse principles to organize economic life, which
need to be described and explained. In this sense, a society's
economy consists of culturally specific processes that its
members use to provide themselves with material resources,
and therefore the economy cannot be considered separately
from the cultural institutions on which it is based. Because
my enquiry seeks to define the cross-cultural perspective of
work ethic, I now examine what is generally accepted as the
concept of work.

Various authors define *economy* as the system of production, distribution, and competition of resources. They
identify the mode of production as a set of social relations
through which labour is deployed to wrest energy from nature by means of tools, skills, organization, and knowledge.
Labour is the activity that links human social groups to the
material world around them; human labour is, therefore, always social labour. Labour can thus be considered the central element in the production process. In a capitalist mode
of production, money buys labour, a process that gives rise

to a division between bosses and workers. Labour is thus a means of production that in nonindustrial societies comes through social links such as kinships structures, marriage, and descent. Although economic systems and motivations are different across cultures, the capitalist worldview operates on the assumption that individuals are motivated by opportunities to maximize profit.

The market principle now dominates most economies, governing the distribution of the means of production, land, labour, natural resources, technology, and capital. Those who lack capital and must sell their labour also lack the means of production. This perspective maintains that humanity's *world* is composed of interconnected processes that are often disassembled into fragments and turned into concepts like *nation* and *culture*, but that falsify reality if they are not placed within their proper contexts. Only if we comprehend these terms as bundles of relationships and reinsert them in the field from which we remove them, can we hope to increase our understanding of the real issues.

In modern industrial societies, social cohesion is mainly expressed through participation in the world of work because work and citizenship are connected to the web of social ties that hold a given society together. The insecurity of a deregulated labour market and the introduction of information and communication technologies in industry have undermined the social contract by threatening the interaction between work and citizenship. During the 1980s in Great Britain, various forms of employment protection were dismantled and the ability of trade unions to protect their members was weakened; this occurred during a massive increase in unemployment, which significantly altered the balance of power between capital and labour. These changes were accompanied by encouragement of enterprise and labour market flexibility, which led to the removal of technical and political barriers between national economies in order to create a unified market for unrestrained international competition.

In nonindustrial societies, a kin-based mode of production prevails. One acquires rights to resources and labour through membership in social groups, not impersonally through purchase and sale. Though Maori generally live and work in an industrial and capitalist system, the proceeds of their labour are distributed through a web of social relations and obligations. It is, therefore, necessary to treat the Maori economy as nonindustrial, because it lacks economic decision making based on the profit motive. Maori economy has traditionally been based on a system of reciprocity, whereby goods are exchanged and services are returned. In contrast, capitalist society involves an exchange of goods calculated in terms of a multipurpose medium of exchange and standard of value—money—and is carried on by means of a supply-demand-price mechanism, or the market. Nevertheless, markets never exist outside a cultural and social context. In the same way that people produce goods and services, they also produce and reproduce interpretations of the productive process and their roles in that process. Marx favoured the term *ideology* to refer to the cultural products of conscious reflection, such as morality, religion, and metaphysics. Other authors have described the ideology that governs the contemporary labour market as *neoliberalism*, the idea that trade and individual choice should not be subject to government regulation.

This neoliberal labour market counterclaims the value systems that compose the work ethic of many workers, as its general trends subject them to liberal ideologies of individualism, self-reliance, individual contract acts, and choices for which they are individually held accountable. Those who see market forces as the primary engine of world improvement use the terms *globalisation* and *development*, which indiscriminately occurs within globalisation. But what do we mean by development? The term tends to refer to processes of social and economic change that are the result of economic growth and specific policies, and that can have either positive or negative effects on people. Many theorists since the 1980s have seen that the radical changes in market ideology over the last two decades have negatively affected many workers due to their inability to swiftly adapt to the ensuing sociocultural and economic changes. This book specifically examines how Maori people have adjusted to changes in the broader socioeconomic systems that have occurred since Anglo-Saxon colonization. Maori men, in particular, have been negatively affected by socioeconomic changes in the New Zealand labour market.

Inconsistencies in the Market

As one of the central themes of my research is a concern with the way that people think about work, it is essential to examine the history of Western and Maori economic activity to determine the circumstances that shaped the belief systems that inform their ideas about work. Understanding developments in machine and information technology over the last three decades will lend insight into the bewilderment of workers who have been affected by changes in their places of work.

New Zealand working conditions in the 1990s have been used as a precedent for labour market changes. At that time, the country's politicians and economists regularly boasted on television and radio that their country was regarded by the rest of the world as a laboratory for the rapid implementation of new market policies and neoliberal ideologies. Much of the information I collected for this study was obtained during my work as a career consultant for a charitable trust in Auckland, where I spoke with people who had been immediately affected by retrenchment and the swift changes that occurred in their workplace conditions.

There is evidence for the claim that the changes in the current labour market represent the way things are, as opposed to what people believe they ought to be according to their work ethic. Such a claim is apparent when people explain how their current work conditions differ from what they were in the past. Yet the claim contains a paradox: recent changes in the world of work are supported by principles and rules that the majority of the workforce has not yet caught up with but are expected to conform to. Due to the accepted notion in Western nations that good citizenship is a consequence of one's willingness to work, inconsistencies arise because one's willingness to work is undermined by a modern labour market that is determined to reduce its workforce. Therefore, job insecurity and joblessness have a direct impact on people's sense of personal identity and way of life. This conflict between the new ideologies of the modern labour market and the traditional work ethic of the Western world and its indigenous and ethnic minorities requires close examination, because workers are caught in the crossfire between technological change and their expectations of participation in the workforce.

To sum up, I have examined the works of various authors whose writings explain the changes that have occurred in the labour market over the last two decades and who have supported their arguments with theories developed on the basis of studies conducted since the onset of the information age. These authors have shown that a change in market procedures and philosophy has taken place, and that drastic transformations in the places of work have affected workplace conditions and employer–employee relations.

The spectrum of beliefs and values that people use to frame their ideas about work are encapsulated in a work ethic that varies between and within societies; it is a result of how people think about their social institutions. Thus, behaviour patterns vary in the world of work as a consequence of worker's differing experiences and their attitudes toward, and expectations of, their participation in economic endeavours. An economy is composed of two realms, the community and the market, which are mutually dependent on the ideational systems that shape the way people think about their social institutions. Culture, not just technology, significantly shapes people's experience and relations in the workplace.

The discussion on the concept of work and work ethic in this chapter shows that there is a conflict of interest between market forces and workers as a result of a change in how the world of work is viewed. The outlook of the Fordist era, with its predictable working conditions and clearly defined workers' rights, has been supplanted by that of the current post-Fordist period, with its globally competitive environment governed by neo-liberalist ideology that promotes individualism, self-reliance, personal accountability, and limited government involvement in trade. This development has created a conflict between the ideology of the current labour market and the traditional work ethic to which workers adhere, a conflict the workforce is still trying to resolve.

Various authors suggest that ideas about work and the expectations of workers are inconsistent with the contemporary realities of labour market ideologies. These inconsistencies can be seen as a result of the expectations of many workers in relation to current market constraints. In this sense, the conditions of the world of work are paradoxical, as they favour the ideology of market processes over the beliefs and norms upheld by the majority of the workforce. Whereas in the Fordist era workers' unsteady and unstable employment conditions were improved by collective bargaining proceedings and union action, the post-Fordist conditions of the market and the individual contract acts have rendered collective agreements a thing of the past. Thus, the new developments in the contemporary labour market have added to a strained relationship between employers and their employees, which may result in a shift from collective beliefs about work to individual sets of principles and norms about work that are more adaptable to change and to objectives that individuals set for themselves. The consequences of the contemporary rules and regulations in the labour market are also manifested in the psychological consequences of distress and insecurities about work.

The idea of a social contract between workers and their society is increasingly undermined by mass redundancies, frequently changing conditions, and employment contracts that are designed to favour employers and limit the rights of employees. Such actions negatively impact people's work ethic, especially when they are trying to comprehend market transformations and come to terms with the idea that job security is a thing of the past. As culture dramatically shapes human experience, life choices, and expectations, changes in the labour market affect the ideational systems of people who work and those who do not. They have impinged on the values and beliefs of indigenous people and ethnic minorities whose ideational systems differ considerably from those in mainstream Western societies.

As my investigation concerns itself with different people's views and experiences in the world of work, I attempt to explain them by placing them in a relevant social and cultural framework. For this purpose I have presented the concept of *meaning* as a social process by which humans attempt to make sense of their world by formulating ideas about it. These ideas can be interpreted and clarified as people shape their actions according to their experiences, which are a result of the cultural context in which they occur. It is in this context that I consider work ethic to be a shifting component of ideational systems, an idea I use to examine the work practices of the Maori people in New Zealand. I also use the term *work ethic* to delineate and explore how they enact their concept of work as distinct from the integrated system of institutions that constitute Maoridom.

Chapter 3
Real Conditions in the World of Work

The conditions in the world of work are paradoxical, in that expectations of workers do not correspond with the reality of conditions in their workplace, as these are constantly changing as a result of companies modifying their economic objectives. Geert Hofstede, a theorist of the 1980s, defines *value* as a broad tendency to prefer certain states of affairs over others; values are *ends* not means, and their desirability is either unconsciously taken for granted or seen as a direct derivation from one's experience or some external authority. In other words, the issue has certain relevance for us and suggests that norms of value deal with a collectivity and are held by the majority. In this context, the conditions of the world of work are paradoxical, as they articulate the ideology of market processes rather than majority-held ideas about work. The trend towards more control and autonomy in one sense but deterioration and insecurity in another is at the root of the ambivalences in the current developments in working time. Volatility in the labour market can be seen in the increase in intermediary activities, such as training stand-by duty, that make it difficult to accurately monitor work hours. These problems also show how workers are weakened and trapped by their personal commitment to work, and that an alternative approach that properly monitors and restricts working hours should be discussed among groups of workers to find methods to increase efficiency other than pressure of work.

However, there is clearly a problem with this suggested solution, as workers are no longer able to bargain for collective conditions in their places of work due to the introduction of the Individual Employment Contract Acts in Australia and New Zealand. This problem can be attributed to differences between the labour organization and regulation of the industrial era and today. In the former, work tended to be experienced at a more universal level of performed tasks, objective working hours, and collective guarantees, while the latter features flexible working conditions with varied employment experiences, more control and autonomy in the workplace, and increased uncertainty in the job market. The latter trend suggests surrender to increased workloads, hours, and the demands of the job, as ambiguity and mass redundancies now constitute working life.

Today's flexible working conditions render collective problem solving among groups of workers impossible, as employees in Australia and New Zealand are coerced into signing individual employment contracts before they begin their jobs. The irony of post-industrial labour relations and conditions may, thus, be ascribed to the shift from collective employment conditions to individual employment contracts and finally to commercial contracts.

The result is that relations between workers and their employers are increasingly strained, and the shift from collective to individual contracts may eventually transform a collective work ethic to an individual work ethic, which would be more adaptable to different work situations and the objectives that individuals set for themselves. Thus, any investigation into work ethic and the impact of changes in the labour market on working people involves listening to what people have to say about their current conditions. My investigation, therefore, emphasizes ideational perspectives of the world of work and the meaning that workers themselves attach to their participation in it.

In the past, work was regulated to promote stability and standardized work hours for all workers. Many of the participants in this study referred to these conditions while expressing their frustration about the current situation in the world of work. The objective of flexible working conditions, diversity of employment situations and experiences, and the demands of personal commitment to company goals and survival, fail as an incentive for people to comply with the rules of the modern labour market, especially in view of continuing mass redundancies.

The relationships between unemployment, poverty, financial strain, and psychological distress have been the subject of surprisingly little empirical research. Employment provides a variety of benefits both manifest and latent, and therefore has profound mental health implications. An analysis of variations in psychological distress by labour force status shows that the major contrast is between those who have work and those who don't. It suggests that the psychological consequences of unemployment and mass redundancies are a widespread problem, as society perceives being out of work as reflecting a person's shortcomings, placing the blame on the shoulders of the unfortunate individual.

Furthermore, unemployment destroys a habitual structure of a fixed time schedule for the working day. Many of my participants commented on having too much time on hand, while others complained that too much time was spent at work as a result of various jobs being collapsed into one task, making the job description amorphous.

People increasingly tend to become personally involved in their work because of various pressures, such as the need to meet deadlines for the success of the company or simply because endless tasks have taken over their lives. These conditions describe the work experiences of management and skilled workers and their problems in managing unduly heavy workloads. Many participants told me that trends in management are spilling over onto the rest of the workers, who are also experiencing increased workloads and time-consuming tasks that impinge upon their private lives. The transition from collective to commercial contracts has contributed to a strictly utilitarian relationship between workers and firms, which may cause a variety of valuable individual and collective skills to be lost for good. The attitudes of participants reflect these new developments in the world of work, especially those that happened the 1990s, when the New Zealand labour market changed at a staggering speed and mass redundancies occurred at almost a daily rate.

Many managers described their experiences at work as stressful. Their stress levels seem to have worsened in having to deal with the contradiction between the need to reduce their own working time and the need to fulfil their responsibilities and meet their targets. Managers tend to make company objectives their own by appropriating and restructuring them into an intensely subjective relationship with their work as they accept unreasonable targets imposed upon them by the organization.

Nevertheless, industrial relations arise out of work and the relationship between workers and employers, a relationship that is fundamental to work conditions. The 1980s saw the rise of the Excellence Movement, which led companies to comb the labour market for charismatic leaders in order to achieve organizational excellence. Human resource management became the means for achieving this goal under what amounted to be a new corporate culture. Companies and managers wanted to be assured that the people they hired were genuinely committed to organizational goals through personal involvement and responsibility for the overall well-being of the company.

However, my study contends that the pursuit of excellence and the objective of transforming employee values and beliefs ignores the fact that in a labour market in which employees are given greater autonomy and responsibility, worker subordination to company rules and dictates cannot be taken for granted, especially when loyalties easily shift to the highest bidders in the market. Employment relations, therefore, tend to expose the disparity between workers' interest in maximizing their income and employers' persistence in minimizing costs and reducing staff numbers, while also insisting that workers be duty-bound to the interests of the company.

The Process of Research

I used qualitative methods to gather information for this book in order to obtain a more detailed understanding of workers' beliefs and feelings about the conditions and reformations in the labour market. Qualitative methods are *interpretive*, or *descriptive*, using descriptions and categories obtained from open-ended interviews, observation, field notes, recordings, questionnaires, and other means. This approach is employed by researchers to study participants in their own environment through informal recorded conversations or note-taking through observation. In the past, participant observation fieldwork was generally carried out in relatively stable and remote communities; today, subjects are less likely to be bounded communities or cultures in remote parts of the world than trans-localities, border zones, or migrant groups. For instance, labour migration research may require observations and interviews in both home communities and distant immigrant camps.

Qualitative research in the social sciences involves an in-depth understanding of human behaviour and the reasons that govern human actions. The strengths of its methods lie in the focus and detail of the interviews and conversations with participants, which may not be possible to obtain in a standardised questionnaire. The researcher is often able to recognize experiences and incidents that may have been overlooked by other researchers; it helps him or her to appreciate these experiences from the worldview expressed by the participants rather than from a perspective that may have been imposed upon them. Its goal is to try to capture what is happening without being judgmental and to represent the view of the participants rather than the interviewer.

However, a problem arose in my research because not everybody was willing to volunteer information about their thoughts and feelings in relation to work. Many participants told me they felt fearful or wary about possible repercussions, such as being recognized by management, or an unemployment agency if they depended on the government for their income. Only the assurance of anonymity, which was included in the questionnaires and interviews, overcame the problem.

I conducted most of the interviews for this investigation during the 1990s, when changes in the world of work occurred at a rapid pace and places of work became insecure or unavailable through mass layoffs. I conducted later interviews through questionnaires over the internet, on bulletin boards, on notice boards, and in online chat rooms. I used the internet and face-to-face conversations to gather data from people whose expectations for continued employment and traditional ways of thinking about work had been shattered by the steady encroachment of new rules in the work place. I gleaned data from conversations in which people described how they felt about the changes in the workforce, what they felt considered their right to work, and how they felt about being deprived of that right when they had been made redundant. This method of providing relevant information can be described as the action of stating and explaining one's position on what are generally controversial issues.

I used questionnaires to gather data from people living at a distance from me, but their usefulness was limited, as I received concise replies tailored to the questions. In contrast, personal interviews generated more questions and created a setting of mutual trust. I taped my interviews with Maori participants, as they preferred to ignore the questionnaires because they regarded the information they offered to be of more importance.

Interviews at the Waipareira Trust Village in Auckland, a primarily Maori social environment, tended to start with some trepidation on the part of the participants. Maori are generally cautious about Pakeha inquiries into their lives. However, they conveyed more information when they realized that I was quite familiar with Maori institutions and ways. The Waipareira Trust Village is managed by Maori workers, volunteers, and a committee, in the Maori tradition.

It contains, among other departments, a WINZ office that can be compared to Centerlink in Australia, and which is also staffed by Maori employees. My participants advised me that, unlike Maori villages in rural areas, this village contained many members of various tribes who worked together for a common goal. I followed cultural observations strictly and attended *karakias* (prayers) before the start of the working day and ceremonies of any kind.

The Research Sites

During the 1990s, I was a member of the Fair Deal Coalition in Auckland. I interviewed union members and listened to their accounts of dwindling membership due to the effects of the Individual Employment Contract Act. This development in the labour market involved a decline and near destruction of unions, which reported a great loss in membership as workers were increasingly forced to sign individual contracts that contained clauses that restricted association with unions. During this period, union delegates were banned from the workplaces, and individual job contracts left workers without bargaining powers.

Workers became well aware of this development and attributed decreased loyalty and bargaining ability to the diminished powers of their unions. They realized that they signed away collective rights in their individual employment contracts and could no longer rely on the backing of collective agreements, which instilled in them a fear of dismissal. As many had been rejected in their applications for jobs elsewhere, they preferred to manage their existing workplace rather than risk losing the job they had.

I collected the major portion of my data from a charitable trust in New Zealand. I had volunteered as a career consultant for a trust in Auckland that had been created by a group of mature and skilled professionals, most of whom who had been made redundant in the early 1990s on the basis of their advanced ages. The group provided a service for others whose skills were valuable and useful but who were discriminated against on the assumption they were too old for the job. Their hurt, frustration, and bewilderment played a great part in their disillusionment towards work prospects and life in general.

I conducted the interviews in forty-five minute sessions, during which I gained considerable insight into the problems workers faced when most of their protections, rights, and guarantees had been undermined. As the clientele of the organization included workers from various cultural backgrounds, I learnt that the concept of work ethic did not mean the same thing to people who grew up outside mainstream society. I recognized a distinct need to investigate the experiences of these groups to gain a more accurate understanding about what people mean when they talk about work and how this institution fits in with other social institutions.

I took considerable steps to ensure that my participants came from a variety of working situations and national backgrounds, so I could gain a better idea of how they conceptualized their roles in the workforce. The provision for anonymity allowed participants to more freely express feelings and grievances about working conditions and employer–employee relations. My participants conveyed a great deal of concern and distrust towards employers as a result of many disappointments and situations in the job market that had given rise to insecurity and inconsistencies. I interviewed both employers and employees, and the sentiments of each were on the opposite ends of the spectrum. But on the whole, both workers and employers expressed that work gave them a reason to get up every morning and that it should provide them with great satisfaction, expectations, and rewards.

As stated earlier, the Waipareira Trust Village was a key site from which I obtained data from Maori participants. I also contacted two Maori elders in Auckland, one of whom was well-known as a political activist who had supported various Polynesian protest movements around the Pacific; the interview with them was conducted at the home of one of them.

I conducted an interview with the manager of a Maori school of technology at his office on the school premises and in his home. Others were conducted in private homes of Maori participants. I also interviewed Maori people who had migrated to and are working in Brisbane to ascertain if working away from their homeland would cause Maori to change their views about work. I interviewed these participants either in my home or theirs. The only difference I was able to observe was that the concept of *whanau* (extended family) has been widened in the migrant community to include not only members of the same *hapu* (sub-tribe), but any friend who happens to be Maori.

I chose to interview my Maori participants in their urban environments because the majority of Maori now reside and work in the cities, where they are subjected to the same rules and regulations of the market as other workers. Work on the *marae* (village centre) and in villages and rural areas is generally carried out in a distinct Maori way, anchored in traditional institutions. All participants had started their lives in rural areas, spoke Maori as their first language, and later migrated to the cities, where they had to adjust to Pakeha institutions, such as the school system. Most of the more mature participants reported that they had been caned at school for speaking Maori. Some related that in the city they were made to feel that being Maori was not desirable, and were discriminated against in the school system and in society.

After conducting interviews, discussions, and questionnaires, I studied texts to support the data collected from participants in order to elicit patterns of ideas, discover the processes in the labour market, and recognize cultural belief patterns. This practice required examining the properties that emerged from relations among things and using keywords in these descriptions to generate deeper interpretation of the meanings of data. Accordingly, I analysed themes that emerged from my readings and interviews to distinguish the processes of the labour market and workers' reactions to changes in conditions, traditional patterns, and ideology. I searched for evidence of social conflict and contradictions in work patterns between the Pakeha and Maori. I looked at how workers expressed their relationships with their employers and why these seemed to have deteriorated. I inquired into the ways people solve current problems in the workforce, and the way employers and workers use their options or fail to resolve them. My analyses are based on the desire to understand people's experiences in as much detail as possible in order to identify categories and concepts that emerged from what I have read and link them to the theories that I used to interpret my data.

To justify my research into the ideational systems of Maori people regarding work and to validate my assertion that culture shapes ideational systems, I begin chapter four with an example from Japan of cultural differences in ideational systems in relation to work, although it can be expected that changes may have occurred in this country's work environment due to changes in social conditions since the time the study was conducted. In order to further substantiate my claims about changes in the labour market, I show how they have affected New Zealand workers by presenting participants' explanations about relationships between employers and employees, focusing on whether they are based on loyalty or distrust and whether the two parties have been able to create workable arrangements. Employers primarily decided to complete questionnaires due to their lack of time; participants on the internet and during subsequent interviews offered additional data on personal experiences. Both employers and workers viewed their relationship with the other as suffering due to divergent ideas and expectations about work. Their contributions enabled me to better understand how market forces and ideologies have changed more quickly than people's ability to manage such changes in their working lives.

Chapter 4
Understanding Ideas about Work

This chapter describes two theoretical frameworks that can be used to understand culturally different approaches to the concept of work. The first was developed by John Dunlop, an author of the late 1950s who argued that the technological characteristics of a workplace and a work community are the result of the environment in which they are placed. However, the viewpoint of Ronald Dore proposed that ideology rather than environment governs the workplace and determines its industrial relations.

Discussion of neoliberal globalisation of the labour market shows that technological innovations in transportation and communication have led to the integration of national markets into a global market in which industrial environments and relations conform to the same rules. Although Dunlop and Dore's theories are rather dated, they are helpful in determining that the neoliberal "one-size-fits-all" model of Dunlop's convergence theory does not have the same effect in reality, because, as Dore argued, it covers existing structures, histories, and cultures. Hence, I have included these two theories to demonstrate how ideational systems are shaped by culture and thus shape people's relations to work. Indeed, the division between Dunlop and Dore's theories of the mid-twentieth century have not converged in terms of objectives to be found in the contemporary world of work.

Following my discussion of Dunlop and Dore's examples, I provide an overview of employers' perceptions of work conditions in New Zealand in order to provide background for the data provided by my Maori participants in later chapters.

Dunlop and Dore's Theories of Work

The dichotomy between Dunlop and Dore's arguments shows that workplace relations are shaped by more complex factors than workplace conditions. Dunlop argued that the technological characteristics of a workplace and work community are the result of the conditions of the environment in which they are placed. He contended that identical environments in quite different societies strongly influence the actors and regulations of industrial relation systems. Dunlop further argued that with similar technological contexts and market constraints for industry, the technological and market contexts are likely to be most influential in putting in place standardized rules that have been adopted by countries with comparable industrial backgrounds. Dunlop alleged that his formal theoretical framework could be applied to studies of workplaces that produce the same goods under identical conditions around the world and that they would yield corresponding results.

Dore, on the other hand, contested Dunlop's viewpoint by arguing that ideology rather than environment governs the workplace and determines its industrial relations. Dore insisted that the system of ideas in a work environment is determined by culture. Dore substantiated his argument by a study he carried out in two virtually identical factories in Great Britain and Japan that produced domestic electric appliances and small motors. Despite nearly identical conditions in manufacturing, their workers did not abide by similar sets of rules. On the contrary, their systems of operation seemed to have developed along lines of different scope and sphere. Dore noted that the differences between the British and Japanese companies clearly surfaced in the concept of lifetime commitment, a striking characteristic of the Japanese employment system, versus the more contractual relationship between a British worker and the company that employs him.

The Japanese system traditionally considered a worker's family to belong peripherally to the company family, whereas the British system sharply separated a man's role as employee from that of husband and father. In Britain, more importance was placed on the actual quality of personal relations within families, while in Japan, concern focused rather on the family as a corporate group in ancestry, honour, and property. According to Dore, the modern Japanese corporation was to be viewed as an extension of the ancient samurai band model, which bound together family groups in a hierarchical network of loyalties and obligations and which subjected families to the fief of the samurai.

Admittedly, the conditions in Japan's industrial system have undergone significant changes since the 1970s to accommodate a globalising labour market and information and communications technologies. But to expect that they have developed along the same lines as, or have converged with, developments in the Western European world of work is unreasonable in view of the variations in the historical and ideological perspectives of the two systems. Dore equated the differences in the British system with the characteristic of individuality, which is hailed as a virtuous quality. In the Japanese firm, on the other hand, the samurai band ideology was passed on to the post-WWII context of work relations and perpetuated in group-centered places of work.

Dore's work suggests that ideas about work are shaped by the culture of the wider society. I acknowledge that there have been more recent studies about Japanese industrial relations and how they fit in the globalising market, but I chose to highlight Dore's work because it demonstrates how differences in labour organizations and work environments are dramatically shaped by differences in culture and the values and beliefs that constitute ideational systems.

The differences between the British and Japanese systems of work were useful in my investigation into cross-cultural differences in work ethic to explain the work experiences and ideals of my Maori participants. The indigenous people of New Zealand became exposed to mainstream Pakeha society when they signed the Treaty of Waitangi in 1840, which was intended by the government to integrate the Maori into their wider society and its economy. Dore's example of the differences in the Japanese and British industrial systems supports Roger Keesing's definition of culture as "those socially transmitted patterns for behaviour that are characteristic of a particular social group." The Japanese example shows that while Japan has been regarded by some as a modern Western country, its industrial relations system demonstrates that the ideas that govern economic activity do not necessarily serve the same purpose and goals, and that the relations between workers and their workplaces are not necessarily based on the same principles. My Maori participants suggested that the values and beliefs that constitute their ideational systems differ in relation to and as a consequence of their experience and participation in the labour market. But what of the labour market generally? What are the changes in the labour market, and how have employers and employees responded to them?

Employers' and Employees' Comments on Work Relations and Conditions

Initially it was difficult to obtain appointments with employers to record their comments on their ideas about work and how they perceive employment relations and conditions in the workplace and the labour market. For that reason questionnaires were sent out to local employers and posted on online notice boards in order to obtain a more balanced perspective of working relations in the market. To safeguard the identities of my participants, their names were changed. I selected Mark's comments as a sample of how an employer of professionals feels about his work and his staff. His comments support various authors' understandings of the positions of managers and employers in the workforce.

Mark's Experience

"As an employer I feel that people have very different attitudes to work nowadays. I believe that, previously, work was chore-based, something that was not enjoyable but necessary, whereas today the focus for many people is more on satisfaction in the job. I admit that this outlook reflects my general environment of relatively well-paid professionals, but that workers on the assembly line at Golden Circle may not necessarily feel the same way.

"I feel that job security depends on the individual in the way he or she manages his or her career in the face of a changing work environment and the need to adapt to these changes. Paid work is still predominant in our social order, as there as yet does not appear to be an alternative to satisfy economic needs in the foreseeable future. Employment relations have changed, as many professionals have greater choice now and are therefore more inclined to leave an employer who does not provide them with what they seek for in the job. On the other hand, employees tend to be more willing to be committed to, and involved in, their work if the opportunity is provided. I feel, therefore, that employers are faced with the fact that in order to attract the best people for their businesses, they need to actively compete in the market."

Mark discussed the situation in his own work environment, which he described as one of "professionals who work with enthusiasm at their tasks in a congenial working climate." Increased hours spent at work by this sector of the workforce tend to be rewarded in other areas, such as being able to work from home or take time off. However, in other sectors of the workforce, workers face dismissal if they cannot work increased hours. This clearly shows the widening gap between the two sides of today's workforce. The demand to meet deadlines for the company in the production of goods and services also means that working men and women experience fewer leisure hours outside work, as their job requirements increasingly make inroads into their private lives.

Mark owns his own business and employs professionals who travel to promote the firm's programs. Mark's comments coincide with those of various authors who have described current ways of thinking in the workplace, and who have argued that the modern industrial model has changed along with ideas about industrial and employment relations. They argue that contemporary ways of thinking emphasise practices that focus on efficient human resource management in order to guarantee that those that are hired are genuinely committed to company goals.

Thus, the pursuit of excellence and the objective of transforming employee values and beliefs ignore that workers' submission to company rules and terms can no longer be taken for granted in a labour market in which employees are given greater autonomy and responsibility and loyalties tend to shift easily to the highest bidders in the market. Employment relationships, therefore, tend to expose the disparity between workers' interests in maximizing their income and employers' persistence in minimizing costs and reducing staff numbers, while also insisting that employees be duty-bound to the interests of the company. Similarly, no company policy can produce results without people to carry out certain tasks. Thus, any attempt in bringing about change in the way that people think about work, through the pursuit of excellence and human resource management, only serves to highlight the fact that if employers wish to attract the best employees, they need to pay more than their competitors in the labour market for skills, loyalty, and reliability.

Mark's comments seem to substantiate the fact that the only way to motivate employees to identify with the company, contribute to its success, and show dependability is to recognise and reward efforts. To ignore the importance of such managerial conditions is to risk losing the best people in the organisation to the competition, or to attract unsuitable personnel for the job, which causes greater staff turnover and loss of productivity. Mark demonstrates that he is well aware of this trend in the labour market and has managed to hire employees who, through just rewards for effort, are happy to be committed to their work.

Unfortunately, this does not appear to be the overall trend. Some employers voiced their frustration about the increased mobility of the workforce. Some believed that workers should have more satisfaction in today's workplace because they now have more responsibility and are allowed to make decisions. Employers did, however, express their awareness that such employees are expensive and that they are pitched against the forces of the market in their search for suitable staff. One employer expressed that it is discouraging to consider that every one of his workers has a life outside the workplace and that no company ever became rich allowing its workers to work only forty hours per week. Another pointed out that personal savings are often tied up in a company and in company stock, and therefore businesses are to make money in whatever way their workers see fit. Although the balance of power has indeed shifted to companies, the sense that workers are still much better off than in the 1980s prevails in this group.

An indignant comment in defence of employers came from the USA. The participant's remarks suggested that he was either an employer or manager, certainly someone with authority. He stated that the issue rested upon the leverage and economics of supply and demand. Those who have the leverage, he insisted, have the power.

> Right now, in some companies, the employees hold the power that runs the industries. These are the technology workers who, because of their exceptional positions, think that they cannot be replaced. For the most part this is true, which is frustrating; these people leave for the slightest thing and the company cannot often find a replacement promptly because of the dwindling numbers in qualified science and engineering graduates.

His views were met with criticism from another well-placed person in the workforce.

> In the past decade, companies have become more concerned with their bottom line and cutting back on a lot of things that used to mean a lot to employees, such as appreciation parties and Christmas bonuses.

Points of view on the nature of work depend on a worker's position and the measure of achievement and monetary rewards they enjoy. Employers and the self-employed certainly expressed a measure of control over their activities and satisfaction over their choice of tasks and rewards. They affirmed that they chose their line of work because they had obtained the necessary preparation for an anticipated career path. They tended to create their own opportunities for growth and development through education and by making things happen for themselves. A participant on the internet compared employers with people who hire rental cars because of their lack of personal interest in or responsibility for their workers, something that would undoubtedly explain the trend of rapid turnover in the workplace.

Workers' Views on Employer–Employee Relations

The workers' views on their relationship with employers were generally pessimistic, especially when they were asked how much loyalty they believe exists on both sides of this relationship. Many commented that loyalty between employers and workers, and work seekers, suffered a setback at the onset of transformations in the labour market when information technology took over many routine tasks. Workers warned that employers should remember the very people they treat with such disdain when they hire and fire at will and anxiously consider the profits they expect to procure from their workforce. Employees reasoned that faith in employers has been replaced by opportunism on both sides, which finds mutual expression in ruthless dismissal on one side and frequent job movement in search of advancement and higher pay on the other. But only those with skills in high demand are able to look for lucrative opportunities. While the majority of the workforce is highly mobile, their mobility is more a result of labour casualization and high dismissal rates rather than employment improvement.

Those who occupy positions that require great skills and training felt more secure in their jobs than those who depend solely on the willingness of an employer to hire them for some unspecified period. Some explained that their work was not what they wanted to do, as they could no longer speak of loyalty in the workplace due to the hire-and-fire mentality of bosses. Some maintained that workers no longer trust their employers because the latter tend to forget those who produce huge profits, which rarely flow down to the workers. Others proposed that workers today have lost faith in their employers and do not award them the same loyalty as they did some thirty years ago. Workers show this by changing from job to job searching for better opportunities and more rewards, rather than staying with one company, as they tended to do in the past. They commented that the reward for helping companies to obtain their sizeable returns is the danger of dismissal. They viewed employers as uncaring about contracts with their staff, because the aims of production weigh heavily on profits and results rather than a fair return for effort.

Paul, a participant who responded from the USA, commented, "Although I know that work is important, I do not feel motivated to do more than what is required of me. I admit that losing my job would have an impact on my lifestyle, but I would rely on other ways to make ends meet rather than look for steady income for a living. As for security in the workplace, I feel that loyalty has left the workplace as a result of the latest dismissal powers of the employers. I feel that there is no loyalty left in the workplace, because workers do not trust their employers anymore because the latter tend to treat them with such casualness and disregard that it becomes difficult to treat their jobs with feelings other than uncertainty and insecurity."

A fifth participant, Nick, was a senior market researcher in the Netherlands. He remarked, "My first thought about work involves income, since it provides a person with the means of self-development. One usually associates the concept of work with obligations and a number of less desirable activities, but everyone hopes that work contributes to the development of self. Unfortunately, jobs that comprise strictly routine activities generally fail to provide these opportunities, although some people are creative enough to add a personal touch to such monotonous tasks.

"In Western societies, too much emphasis is being placed on paid work as being the norm, with the result that people get slotted into status levels on the basis of their earnings. I feel that worker and employer relations have moved from a seller–workers situation to a buyers–employers market; in other words, the force of gravity has changed in the market, seemingly to favour those who hire workers. In response, labour conditions have also shifted from previously stable to presently volatile and insecure situations as a result of frequent job changes. It appears that the relations in the workplace between workers and their employers resemble a tug-of-war between two parties with opposing interests, due to increased competition in the market and technology, which has affected a work ethic to which most workers prescribe but which has become superfluous in an economic system in which labour has become expendable and profit making is paramount. Employers are accused of indifference towards workers' objections against increasing workloads and the formers' powers of dismissal when current conditions in the workplace are not considered to be of acceptable standards."

The sixth participant, Bill, also lives in the Netherlands. His comments were commensurate with those that others made on the effects of the changes that are still occurring in a globalising market.

"The workers of today have lost faith in their employers and, therefore, do not grant them the same loyalty as they did some thirty years ago. The workers show this by easily changing from job to job in their search for better opportunities and rewards. Socially conscious employers who care for their workers have become a rarity, as their pursuit for power and profits has become the focus of ambitions today. You ask me if my opinion reflects a general trend among contemporary workers, and I have to say that it is my impression that workers are less involved in their jobs today. They are a great deal more mobile than before because of the disinterest shown by employers who can, in one move, drastically reduce the numbers of their staff or move jobs, or even entire factories, offshore to countries where labour is cheaper.

"During the last decades the whole situation between workers and employers has degenerated due to increased competition in the market. But then again, since the start of the Industrial Revolution, the ordinary worker has always struggled in the labour market as he had nothing to sell but his labour, unlike the bosses who possess the means of production and who managed to influence governments in their own interests."

Some participants addressed the indifference demonstrated by employers who do not listen to objections against additional and often unpaid workloads and dismiss the workers if they refuse to accept certain conditions. However, one argued against this claim by pointing out that, in his opinion, workers have always refused to accept wages that are not in line with the hours and nature of their work. His remarks were refuted by another discussant, who insisted that for someone who enters full-time employment as a professional, such reasoning would not be helpful, as it depends on the company one works for and the conditions that are agreed to. He stated that if overtime were eliminated, wages would not be increased to reach a desired level, especially since so many people in the market are willing to work for a lot less.

The seventh participant asked why people complain bitterly about the hardships of workers when the problems are so obviously created by consumers. He argued that society's concern appears to be with keeping the family unit of mum, dad, and the children intact, but reduced pay makes it necessary for parents to stay on the job for longer hours, which forces them both to join the workforce and leave children in the care of nannies and other caregivers. The eighth participant insisted that since he was his own master, the issue of the relationship between him and his boss rose and fell according to whether he got the job done.

The ninth participant commented that the principles of loyalty, honesty, commitment, and stability were meaningless in today's world, as established businesses had radically altered their management methods to keep up with market demands and profit margins. He explained that he was a retired craftsman and was very pleased to be out of his line of work, as he felt that people no longer wish to pay for genuine handcrafts and customer loyalty has become unreliable.

A tenth participant referred to the transient loyalty of employers by citing the example of three of his friends who, after between twenty and thirty years of loyal and hard work for their respective places of work, had been forced into early retirement to make way for cheaper labour. He stated that because of the "almighty dollar," employers are generally more unscrupulous toward their workers today than ever before.

A retired nurse, the eleventh participant, commented on the topic of loyalty between employer and staff in the same dejected manner, claiming that there was no longer any employer loyalty and that perhaps there never had been any. She had worked in various hospitals and reported that the tendency to hold staff responsible for anything that happens has always been part and parcel of hospital work, even in situations over which the nurses had no actual authority or control. She said, "Workers are always the blame for what management or the doctors decide; sometimes we are caught in the middle and are blamed for things that go wrong on both sides."

Indeed, I received a number of responses from other participants who argued that companies are concerned with workers' rights only when it suits them. The sentiments expressed by both employers and workers clearly demonstrate that feelings of trust and loyalty are disappearing between them. Another discussant stated that there was a lack of faith concerning the social contract between parties. "Those who entered the workforce during the 1990s may well be of the opinion that such loyalty never existed, irrespective of what older workers and employers have experienced."

Many reports, press articles, and media programs have commented on the alleged disappearance of trust and loyalty between employers and employees. The question of whether loyalty and obligations are still being honoured is pertinent in view of the feelings of disillusionment that workers show as a result of mass layoffs and the disregard for long-term employment and loyalty toward companies.

Employers are equally frustrated with frequent staff turnover, which affects productivity. As a result, many companies have moved many of their routine tasks outside the firm or offshore to escape labour costs and disputes in the workplace. Leading enterprises are focusing on the central core of their business—such as product design and marketing—while subcontracting and contracting out anything that they feel is unlikely to provide a return. They argue that there are many economic and social reasons for subcontracting and contracting out; cost may be the initial reason, but by focusing on their core business, enterprises can also rid themselves of the short-term constraints of employment.

The personal interviews demonstrate that the individualization and casualization of the workforce have been factors in transforming workplace relations into an association of suspicion and reserve. Insecure conditions have fostered disloyalty on both sides and disrespect for a work ethic, which previously guaranteed the social inclusion of all parties and their rights. The "time is money" aphorism has given rise to an illegitimate quantification of time and wholesale confiscation of workers' hours outside the working day, further proof of the powerlessness in the bargaining position of workers. Indeed, several participants on the internet mentioned compulsory overtime as an unreasonable demand from employers who are reluctant to hire more staff in view of a possible fall in profits.

Conditions in the labour market seem to change on a regular basis. The question is, how much loyalty has remained in the workplace, and how much of the work ethic is left? Many of my participants agreed that changes in the labour market have affected employer–employee relations, which purportedly were characterized by a measure of loyalty and goodwill on both sides before the introduction of information technology. The resulting transformation of the labour market allegedly led to the deterioration of relations between the parties in the labour arena, which became a breeding ground for feelings of distrust, disloyalty, and seeming disregard for fairness and equity. This relationship has weakened significantly in the industrial climate of profit making, individualization, and insecure job prospects. The argument that the workers of today are better off in positions of more responsibility and autonomy, and are therefore given greater opportunities for self-fulfilment, appears to be negated by longer hours spent at work with no suitable reward. It does not account for loss of social life and the increased strain on families in which both parents need to enter the workforce in order to sustain a certain lifestyle or even to survive. Increased working hours take their toll on family life, a situation that has been examined by current affairs television and talk radio programs that draw the attention of their viewers and listeners to the plight of dysfunctional families in the community. My research suggests that self-fulfilment and responsibility in the workplace are generally enjoyed by those employees who have had access to higher education in order to obtain skills that are in great demand in the market, or those who are employers themselves and are in a position of power or authority over their workforce.

Although professional and highly skilled workers appear to have a certain degree of job security and prospects, the majority of the workforce does not find itself in this category, especially with their jobs being outsourced to other service agencies or offshore. Added to this situation is the problem of discrimination against more mature workers in favour of those who are considerably younger, regardless of tenure or work experience. Conversely, those who have skills that are in high demand prove to be a rather slippery commodity to their employers, as the latter tend to lose them to competitors. An interesting question remains as to how those who are not part of mainstream Western societies experience work and workplace relations.

People from different cultures create ideational systems and organize work and work relations according to the beliefs and values of their society. The next chapter describes Maori people's ideational systems, which include their distinct values and beliefs about work and situates them in the context of a history and culture that predates European arrival by approximately nine centuries.

Although the majority of Maori people were forced to migrate to the cities in search of work during the 1960s and integrate into mainstream institutions, their ideas about work and the value of their contribution to society can be most effectively understood when viewed through the prism of their distinctive ideational system—in other words, through their own perceptions about life and work.

Chapter 5
Maori People in Aotearoa (New Zealand)

This chapter provides an overview of the history of the Maori people in New Zealand, together with an assessment of their values and belief systems, in an attempt to contextualize their responses to my questions, our conversations, and my understanding of their ways.

Much has been written about the history and culture of Maori people in New Zealand and the debate about how the land is labelled, which Walker described in 1990 as "*ka whawhai tonumatou*, struggle without end." However, little inquiry has been made into how the Maori people express their values and beliefs about the rewards they expect for their economic efforts and the goals that they hope to realize in life. Hence, I distinguish between what is generally accepted as the Western work ethic and the ideational systems that shape Maori economic activity within the framework of their traditional ways of being. As I have given a brief history of the Western work ethic in previous chapters, I will now provide an overview of Maori people's history from the times of their arrival in New Zealand in order to provide a context for my discussion about their social and economic lives.

Although the Western work ethic was founded upon the teachings of John Calvin, the modern labour market no longer embraces its religious and historical aspects, as these have moved to different social arenas in Western cultures. In contrast, my participants suggest that Maori religion, and all other aspects of their social life, merge into a mutually conclusive whole as actions in one area call upon the involvement of other facets of their culture, such as the invocations of blessings from God or ancestors on their daily actions and experiences. My participants clarified these fundamental differences in attitude between Pakeha and Maori social characteristics because I had observed their religious practices when participating in activities that support Maori work modes. Here, religious practices need to be placed in the context of the contemporary New Zealand Pakeha industrial system in order to portray the dissimilarities that exist between Maori and Pakeha work experiences and procedures.

To better understand contemporary Maori cultural practices, a description of Maori society and the way its members perceive the origins of their world is helpful. *Taha Maori* (Maori) identity, according to my participants, is a social concept based on descent from the indigenous inhabitants of Aotearoa, who regard themselves as *tangata whenua* (the people of the land). In this context, Maori identity is defined in a tripartite sequence of myth, tradition, and history, which means that gods, ancestors, and living people are linked through genealogical descent patterns and provide Maori with a holistic view of the world in which they live.

The Maori kinship system bounds family members together in economic units that use all resources jointly. Living close to nature imbues the Maori with an inherent view that everything in his or her environment has *mauri* (life force), which needs to be accorded respect and cared for in the same manner as the members of the *whanau* (extended household), *hapu* (subtribe), and *iwi* (tribe). Maori recognize and revere *mauri* in people, and all other living things are consequential to the laws of *tapu* (cosmic power), which demand that Maori hold in highest esteem all nature, as it links them through genealogical paths. These elements of Maori culture are fundamental to understanding the ways that Maori think about their world and their place in it.

Anne Salmond, a social anthropologist, confirms that *tapu* was the source of all creation and that, like the concept of *mana* (authority or power), it travels through all the pathways of descent as each form of life comes together with another to make something new within a network of kinship links. Consequently, the Maori economy was based on strict rules of *tapu*, and every man in Maori society had some degree of personal *tapu*, which varied with rank and became more intensive as importance increased, as in the case of chiefs. Cooked food and everything associated with it is the very antithesis of *tapu*, and contact with it was sufficient to destroy the *tapu* of any man. Therefore, cooking and collecting firewood was left to slaves, who had lost their *tapu*, and women who had never had any, being *noa* (non-tapu or unrestricted), because a man's back and head are the most *tapu* on his person.

The principles of *tapu* and *noa* are important considerations for the division of labour in the Maori world, as they continue to play an essential part in work practices; they provide a crucial insight into the role of Maori men and women in the workplace. My participants explained why it is difficult for Maori men to work in environments other than those of the collectivities in the freezing, road, and electric works where Maori work closely together in groups. Difficulties also arise for women who work outside their groupings in factories.

The concept of *tapu* must be considered together with that of *mana*, as it too dates back to the culture and language of pre-European Maori, although Maori understanding of it may have changed since their exposure to Christianity and European ways. Alice Metge explained that *mana* means spiritual power and authority, and this divine power is not only manifested through human experience but also in other natural species and places. *Mana* has a double aspect of authority and power and is bestowed by the gods upon humans who act on their behalf to carry out their will. Such agency must not be abused, as it may result in it being withdrawn. *Mana* is held not only by individuals but also by entire descent groups. Therefore, *mana* as spiritual power is closely linked with *tapu*, and those who are *tapu* have *mana*.

The *mana* of the group supersedes that of the individual in importance and, therefore, one is taught to never raise oneself above the group but to work together and contribute to the whole to prevent the social structure from collapsing. This aspect of *tapu* and the interplay of the principles with *mana* is manifest in what the Pakeha mockingly refer to as the "tall poppy syndrome." My participants explained it as a system that actively discourages individual ambition for personal gain and instead advocates the *whanau* organization as the vehicle for collective economic advancement. Hence, *mana* is a moving force, whereas *tapu* is a state of being. These two principles must be understood and explained, as they remain an intrinsic part of Maori people's beliefs and values. A discussion of the Maori work ethic or economics is not worthwhile if it ignores these salient principles, as they feature in the explanations of my participants on how they regard their place in the world of work.

A discussion of the way Maori view their economics in mainstream society must involve their feelings and sentiments about their land and the systematic loss of their holdings. The devastating system of land purchasing, more so than war and confiscation, disrupted the lives of Maori, and the process of colonial plunder was a consequence of Maori and Pakeha objectives being directly opposed in the contest for land, resources, and power. The spiritual and symbolic significance of tribal land in Maori and tribal identity are encapsulated in the Maori adage "man perishes but the land remains." The Maori see the land as a permanent resource to be handed down to succeeding generations, a place where one's spirit has footing, *turangawaewae*. If it is taken away, one loses one's *mana*.

Landlessness has been the major cause for the shift of a majority of rural Maori to the urban centres. The effects of urbanization are clearly visible in city-born Maori, who became, to a certain extent, alienated from the language, culture, and customs of their forebears. Nevertheless, notwithstanding the pressures for Maori people to assimilate into Pakeha New Zealand society and culture, Maori have continued to maintain their identity while successfully adapting to Pakeha institutions to suit their own purposes.

Walker's comments on the Maoris' partial integration into urban life and their retention of a specific and separate identity are important in considering the cultural significance of their work ethic. These comments clearly separate Western ideology, which deals with the here and now in the constructs of a modern labour market, from a Maori ideational system, which guides them into the future always with a backward glance to the past, or as they express themselves, "We walk into the future backwards." In other words, where modern Westerners tend to concentrate on modern technology and use it to further their prospects in the present in order to secure a desirable future, my Maori participants suggested that they do not rely on such means to consider future options, but instead turn to their descent group, specifically their elders, who remind them of how things were done in the past and advise accordingly.

The strands of Maori life were woven together in exchanges of gifts and mutual assistance. They were based on the principles of *utu*, which demanded payment in kind, whether in kindness or revenge, and were subject to the laws of *mana* and *tapu*. In contrast, the activity in Western societies called work began to occupy a central position in our overall perception of the meaning and purpose of daily life. Modern capitalism saw the emergence of competitive individualism and entrepreneurialism, which can be interpreted as an inevitable consequence of the growth of the cult of the individual, in which personal success and individual ambition have displaced the more traditional and communal forms of economic motivation.

In modern thinking about work, personal knowledge and education became valuable assets with which to transcend social barriers in favour of material and economic achievement aided by technological invention. Maori people's system of exchange caused them to struggle in an environment in which survival of the fittest in the struggle for access to valuable resources was a way of life. Maori people had been isolated in their own environment for centuries before the arrival of British colonizers and had developed their own distinct culture. Despite their ensuing exposure to the institutions and situations of their Pakeha counterparts, dissimilar sets of preconceptions gave rise to largely different conclusions. Thus, to assume that Maori industry is motivated solely by a desire for material goods will lead to conclusions that are far removed from the realities of Maori life.

Tapu and Mana

In discussing the values and belief systems that govern Maori economic activity, it may be asked why the principles of *tapu* and *mana* should be considered salient factors in labour market practices and beliefs. It must be understood that these laws underpin all Maori social and economic action; it is these ideas that my participants explained in their accounts of the practices of work and society in Maoridom.

The working population, traditionally and to a certain extent today, was strictly divided into men who were *tapu* and women who were *noa*. Cooked food, kitchen work, and gathering of wood, were, as I described earlier, off-limits to men, whose contact with these items or their environment could destroy the *tapu* of any part of their person. In order for men and women to enjoy food together as a community, the *tapu* of the cooked food has to be lifted ceremoniously by a *tohunga* (Maori priest) or an elder of the tribe. These matters are clarified in the interviews with my participants in this and the following chapters; they describe how Maori ideas on work and the community are in great contrast to Pakeha perceptions. My participants told me that in order to gain insight into the Maori way of life and their institutions, one cannot avoid the principles of *tapu* and *mana*, or the way in which the *whanau* principle dominates all social considerations and extends into the world of work. Hence, these aspects of the social and economic organization of the

Maori people must be included in discussions about their work behaviour and practices.

Ways of Working

When interviewed for comments on the work habits of Maori, mainstream New Zealanders tended to denigrate Maori people's efforts by listing their problems as a haphazard commitment to the job, a seeming lack of concentration on the task at hand, and an apparent detachment from the workplace itself. While Pakeha perception suggests that there are distinct driving forces operating at work, we may also accept that Maori economic effort is but a part of all activities in their society. In other words, there is a strong indication that the job does not take centre place in life for Maori people in the way that it does for workers in mainstream society.

On the other hand, Maori retort that Pakeha do not take care of their obligations to extended family and that their ambitions are directed by the almighty dollar in the pursuit of material goods. In Maori society, other things may take priority over a job, such as a *tangi* (funeral), for instance, which requires all relatives to be present, irrespective of the day of the week, whether one needs to be at work or not, or even if the absence at work may jeopardize one's job. Such Maori priorities baffle many Pakeha, who then find reason to label Maori workers as lazy or easily distracted from their obligations to their places of work.

Raymond Firth, regarded by many as an authority on Maori economics, stated that Maori people used to perform tasks that require intensive labour, such as sheep shearing and tree felling. Such tasks, until recent times, were performed by groups of Maori men who worked together in forestry, the freezing works, and on the roads, where fathers, sons, brothers, and cousins worked together. An important factor in their incentive to work could be their need to work in the company of other members of the *whanau* or *hapu*.

Most aspects of Maori culture offer emotional support to Maori, something that Pakeha fail to understand. Pakeha values, generally, rest on the principles of money, home, the job, or commodities, whereas Maori argue that they survive mostly on spirituality and the spiritual things attached to their Maoritanga. My research supports the contention that the spheres of economic effort and ambition among Maori people are different from those of the Pakeha, favouring one set of beliefs above those of the other in an unequal struggle for survival. Distinctive political, religious, and linguistic habits all reflect certain values, ideational paradigms, and bodies of knowledge that guide and regulate interaction between human beings. Therefore, institutions founded upon them cohere in important and complex ways that usually reinforce and guide economic practices.

By the third decade of the twentieth century, the Maori had been predominantly absorbed into European society through intermarriage and serious efforts of consecutive governments to integrate them into the mainstream world. Maori people were encouraged to turn away from their own language and customs and to adopt a European lifestyle based on the idea of individual ownership of land and regular employment. This policy promoted the idea that equal opportunity, and reward according to performance, would prove that Maori failure was a clear result of personal lack of effort. However, the key to success in a modern labour market depends on education and skill training, and efforts in this area seemed to be continuously doomed to failure, for reasons my participants offer in the following chapters.

According to Snook's writings, this phenomenon existed because Maori education consisted of practical learning and oral instruction, and did not take place in a structured setting. This style of education was supplanted by British education structures and a written system. Indeed, Donna Awatere, a Maori female activist during the 1970s and 1980s, maintained that in 1840 the Maori chiefs could not have foreseen the demise of their people, and that the land and fisheries were to pass into Pakeha hands. Defeatist attitudes then replaced Maori pride in their culture and language when they were forced to adopt the Anglo-Saxon way of life. Technically and legally, Maori enjoy the same rights to further their economic interests, but due to a range of social and economic barriers, including the Pakeha system itself, the mainstream education system has failed Maori children because of differences in their modes of learning and the denial of their right to express themselves in their own language.

Although disparities between Maori and Pakeha in economic power are substantial, Maori do not tend to compete with the Pakeha for a share in material wealth, as it is not accorded priority above the basic values of love, respect, and sharing. Since the focus of Maori economic pursuit seems to be community welfare rather than individual interest, Maori workers find it difficult to cope with the rules and regulations of a capitalist economic structure, which dictates that days taken off to attend a *tangi* or any other significant event on the *marae* are against the interests of the workplace. A participant noted that Maori do not seem to be overly concerned with the Pakeha idea of investment in the future, as sharing with those around you is of chief consideration. As he remarked, "Fulfilling one's duties and obligations to the members of your village and *hapu* add *mana* and strength to your position in the order of the *marae*." Worrying about the future is superfluous and beyond the immediate care of home and family. The differences in attitude towards work reflect the dissimilarities between spiritual and secular rewards, or the social and economic spheres in which the two economic systems are set, which seem difficult to bridge.

The Maori people are ready to admit that migration from rural areas to urban centres has forced them to become dependent on the capitalist system for survival. Yet it appears that the anticipated assimilation and integration of Maori into mainstream institutions and ways of life have had the opposite result: an intensified awareness of a separate Maori identity, with clearly differentiated outcomes for economic expectations and participation. Although Maori have been under considerable pressure to conform, they have maintained their particular relationship with the natural world and ethos, as the force of tradition remains strong and many phases of economic and social acts are observed with the appropriate ceremonies and rituals of *karakia* (prayer) and *tapu* considerations.

In this and the following chapters, my participants explain what work means to them and how it fits with their broader social institutions. They also explain how Maori men and women view their roles in mainstream society, giving accounts of how the rule of *tapu* works to restrict many Maori men from full participation in the Pakeha world, where they are required to work side by side with women or may be subject to female authority, which is seen to diminish their *mana*. The chapters also offer an account of how some Maori women have made inroads into the Pakeha system sufficient to promote programs for the care of Maori women and children and Maori prison inmates, because Maori women are *noa* and are not restricted by the social obstacles that Maori men must face.

Maori People's Beliefs and Work Practices

Maori ideational systems, which incorporate their values and beliefs about work, are linked with the descriptions that Maori participants provide about their work practices. Both are portrayed to demonstrate their variation from the ideational systems and work practices of Pakehas in mainstream New Zealand society and in the Western world generally. In the following chapters, I present my Maori participants' points of view rather than rendering an analysis on their behalf without their input. I carefully selected participants from among acquaintances and strangers from various walks of life, from those brought up in the Maori tradition on the marae to those who came from a predominantly urban setting. The participants were volunteers who were aware of the study's objectives and were willing to contribute their knowledge and perspectives. The material gained from the interviews contains religious convictions and practical observations, further confirming my proposal that, in relation to work, ideational systems in Maoridom intrinsically connect thought and action.

I also obtained information from a questionnaire that I placed on a Maori website. However, respondents were reserved in their replies, perhaps for fear that the information could be traced back to them and cause repercussions at work or, for those out of work, with Social Welfare (WINZ). It is for this reason that I gave my participants fictitious names.

This chapter records the information, opinion, and life experiences of the first participant, *Adam*, who consulted the questionnaire at first but opted to offer his personal opinions about the way he viewed his world, which he skilfully placed in a seemingly timeless episode, moving back and forth between the past and the present. I designed the interviews to create an atmosphere in which both parties felt on familiar ground and sufficiently relaxed, without the restraint of formalities or scepticism.

My interview with Adam at the Waipareira Trust Village began with Adam's claim that he is a descendant of Chief Te Kooti, who lived in the Taranaki area on the west coast of the North Island during the Maori wars of the 1860s. At the start of the interview, Adam asked if he could offer a prayer and then proceeded to pray in Maori before continuing in English. After that, I turned on the tape recorder and we settled down to the interview.

I preserved the language Adam used as much as possible in order to convey his thought patterns and prevent the loss of meaning and style. My questions are presented in short italicized sentences or paragraphs, whereas Adam's responses are fully recorded.

Adam had attended the Mormon Church College in Hamilton, New Zealand, and as a result had a good basis for further skill development. During the interview, it became evident that he had good knowledge of other cultures, which served him in dealing with people other than Maori without losing his position in his own cultural context.

In order to comprehend the concept of *awhi mai te whanau*, a principle that Adam and other participants refer to in the interviews, it is necessary to explain the centre place of the *marae* in Maori society. Walker clarifies that the *marae* is an institution that has persisted from pre-European society and, together with its ancestral meetinghouse, remains the focal point of all common activities. The structure of the meetinghouse itself represents a founding ancestor whose carved figure graces the gable of the roof. The *tuhuhu* (ridge pole) depicts his backbone, and the *heke* (rafters) form his ribs. The carved *pou pou* (posts) around the walls of the meetinghouse represent famous ancestors, tribal gods, and culture heroes. Thus, the assembly of the tribe in the meetinghouse on the *marae* has the character of the people meeting together within the bosom of recent and ancient ancestors and gods. As meetings can take place over hours, mattresses are laid out on the floor of the meetinghouse to allow people to sleep.

The Interview with Adam

What are your thoughts about work, how do you view your place in the workplace, and what are your goals and objectives regarding your participation in the workforce?

My first thoughts are for my children, that I can take care of them, that others won't brand them poor because they have to wear hand-me-downs, but that they can be proud of the fact that their father is involved in the youth program as a teacher at the Wai [trust village].

At present I do not have a job in the workforce, but I tell others, "Look, you guys, you have your network, keep your ear out for vacancies of positions." It is good to be in the *whanau way* [extended group of Maori contacts] here and to have their trust and support. But sometimes the opportunity of working with Pakehas means getting into higher levels of work achievement than just working locally for someone who is a labourer himself. You know, if people are happy digging with a shovel in the dirt, that is fine. As for me, I set my goals higher. I have the skills and have no problem telling people that.

There is a structure that I believe in, this is how I see my world. When we first arrived from Hawaiiki [the Maori people's homeland in the East according to their origin stories], there was a definite structure in Maori society.

[Adam proceeded to draw a triangle and divide it into five segments to explain his own interpretation of Maori society.]

At the top of our *whanau* there was God, nobody else. There was God, the God we believed in. The level underneath it contained all the chiefs. Underneath them were the *tohunga* [priests], who are really the guardians. The next level down finds the warriors, and at the bottom there are the ordinary villagers. Now, I don't want to be a villager, I don't want to be a *tohunga,* nor do I want to be a fighter. I want to be a leader, unlike other people who don't realize that they don't always have to pick *kumaras* [sweet potatoes], that they could be the ones who plan where the *kumaras* are to be planted. At Church College I took what was important to me and the rest was discarded. I believe that it is important what other races have to say for your betterment, but if you go too far into their beliefs, you lose your own identity.

A Maori computer class instructor expressed regret that because of his university degree and profession he had lost touch with his village and no longer held the right to speak on the marae. *Might you find yourself in the same position having attended Church College?*

No, because I kept in touch with both sides. While I was learning I was still back with my people. They knew exactly what path I took. I made quite clear to them that I wanted to achieve this and that I wanted to achieve it for Maoridom. I am not doing it for me. I wanted to achieve it for my family in the first place and then for the wider society, not the other way around.

Working in a Pakeha environment means that you get paid for a good day's work. Working for a Maori environment means that you get lazy. The first thing that we want is to be friends, and then we charm people into working. We are known around the world as the friendly Polynesians, and some of our people still think the same way instead of standing up and saying, "No, I don't accept X amount of dollars, I think that with my skills and my outside study, you are getting a good worker." Instead of doing that, they accept anything they are told or given, which is their way. Pakehas, on the other hand, are rather stand-up guys when they say that they want to be hired in the normal way. That is the way I like to be because of the skills I have obtained.

Does this way of thinking differ from the way that your elders on the marae *think?*

No, this is the way these fellas think. Let me tell you a story [he points to the top of the triangle] about the people from the Nga Pui tribe. My dad is Tuhoe from Whakatane. During the Kingitanga Movement in the time of King George [the Maori King Movement in the Waikato region during the 1870s], some chiefs went up to Kauwa Kauwa onto the *marae* and said, "Look, we want you people of Nga Puhi to join the Kingitanga." However, the chief of that *marae* suggested that his guests would have something to eat and then sleep on the matter. He would let them know about his decision in the morning. This *marae* is one of three that are still standing that have a loft in them. When all had gone to sleep, the Nga Puhi chief got up and ordered a slave to sleep in his place. The chief crept upstairs and slept in the loft. In the morning he came down for breakfast. The other chiefs came to him, and the Tanui chief asked him about his decision. The Nga Puhi chief replied, "Last night I slept above you, I was closer to God and I talked to Him. I could not feel his spirit on you and that is why I will never be subject to you."

That is why we were never part of the Kingitanga. And so, like these chiefs, I negotiate with men. I have done things the Pakeha way, but I can still converse in the Maori way. Why should I go backward, why should I go back and plant *kumaras*?

We work by seeing and touching—we have to see somebody who is real, then you must show them clearly the path you must take up the mountain. If you let the grass grow over this path, you no longer see the way back clearly. So it is always a matter of going back and mowing the grass of your paths. It is a matter of *awhi mai te whanau* [embracing and helping your family]. You put your hand out and pull someone through with you. Yes, you are always in the company of others, you always take your *whanau* with you. I always go back to our *kaumatua* [elders] and say, "This is what I am doing, Uncle. What do you think of that?" I sit down with them and discuss with them what I am doing. They always tell stories of the past and I try to relate them to my present situation. I'll sit down with them again two days later and tell them of my decision. So it is not a matter of climbing up alone, but utilizing your people to push you up the ladder. Because who brings you down too? The very same people! They are the same who drag you back down from the ladder. In order to move up, you bring them with you. You hold them and they actually help you to get up there. Tall poppies shoot up, but they may tumble down too. They have their own vision and that is fine. But some things are very strong for Maori, and that is *awhi mai te whanau*—hold onto, hug your family.

As a Maori, do you feel that your people fit in a globalised market? You have had education, but there are many Maori who have not, and they may not have any idea of what is going on. How may they survive in a modern labour market?

Modern labour market? As far as the Maori people, the non-skilled, they will always be on the benefit [social welfare]. They make skilled living out of *street living*. That means that besides the benefit they will do thirty hours a week for an under-the-table job to supplement their income. Living on the benefit actually demands skill, you know. They actually know more of WINZ than the staff themselves know. What they lack in knowledge about paperwork and stuff, they make up by knowing how WINZ operates, and that is being streetwise! They know how to make extra money under the table in such a way that the government cannot find out. It is a skill to market yourself without having a high standard in reading or writing and to be still able to sell yourself as a good worker under the table. Not being able to read or write does not mean that you cannot be a good worker. CVs show their inefficiency. Maori are shy of men with ties on, but they can talk to a man on a one-to-one basis in order to be given a try—it is something that has to come back to give people a chance to work. Maori have to feel you and touch you, they have to feel your *wairu* [spirit] coming from you, they have to know where you want them to work and what needs to be done.

What about job loss? How does it affect a Maori person or his family, or his or her status on the marae?

If you are a chief [in pre-European times] and you would fail in your duties, you would be killed, end of story. If the people did not like you, they would not sack you, they would kill you. If you lost your job as a *kumara* picker, it did not matter, you became the babysitter, you were already down there. This is the status that I am talking about.

It depends on what position you held in your job and for how long and how you lost it—the immediate focus would be on how you handled yourself. If you were a leader in an industry and you were way up there and you got pulled over for theft, people talk and that is the pressure state. Now, if your firm moved to Brisbane and the local plant is shutting down, you take your redundancy package, you retain your *mana*. A worker of no outstanding position in the *whanau* structure is pulled straight back into the family: "Don't worry about it, mate, you can go and look after the kids. You cannot plant *kumaras*, but you are good with the kids. Away you go." But you cannot tell a chief to look after the kids. It all depends on how we lose that job as to how we will react.

Being able to speak on the *marae* also depends on how you lost your job. If you are a chief and you resigned because of a possibility of having the police involved in your actions, that really is a *mana* puller—you might not want to speak on the *marae* after that shame. You always have the *makatu* [stigma] of it. You always have the *makatu* because your family will always be known for what you have done. People are still wearing the brand of Takatu Wakanene, some chief who did something, and I am the worst one for always bringing this incident up when I see his descendants on our *marae* by telling them that their ancestor was a traitorous pig.

How do you feel that your young people prepare for work? Do you think that your elders still have influence over them, or have they lost them?

No, they have been told to leave them alone. Values have gone out the door and have been replaced with something called money. *Kaumatua* can only give advice to anyone who sits with them and listens. It is a matter of wanting to sit on a piece of grass, like I used to do, and listen to stories about people who are dead. The parents have lost the old values—even the ones around the *marae* have gone that way.

I showed you that our world is consistent and that I am talking about Maoridom in general, all right? Here is God, the chiefs, and the people [he points to the triangle he drew]. The Europeans came in and turned our perfect triangle upside down: "We don't want your gods, called *Tangaroa* or whatever, forget your own gods." They put God at the bottom. "Your chiefs are now under us, and your carvings are disgusting—put clothes on them," and they turned our world upside down. Then they made what you call *poupou* [posts] to stabilize the upturned triangle. A post on one side is called *money*, one on the other is called *alcohol*. Then there is one called *car*, and the last one is for WINZ. WINZ is part of that picture now. To balance the structure on a point like that you have to have the poles in place to hold it steady. Now, what happens if Maori get on the benefit? The pole starts leaning and they call us unbalanced. So we must do something to hold that *poupou* up. When we get on the alcohol, the world gets unbalanced. When our car gets re-possessed, we are unbalanced. When we lose our job, unbalanced again. And this is what I believe is happening. They colonized us, end of story. They upended our world and put our gods at the bottom.

In what ways do you consider that the education system functions in Maori society? How would you explain the phenomenon that at the turn of the twentieth century there was one hundred percent literacy among the Maori people?

It was sixty years since the Treaty of Waitangi. We wanted literacy for the injustices that were done to us, and so it was passed from *marae* to *marae*: "Get someone in there, we want to keep this treaty alive and we want to put these injustices down on paper." So people did get up there and did it—they learned to read and write. If you failed to record events, the consequences were swift and thorough, you were finished, the Pakeha would wipe out your tribe: "How dare you say something against us?"

Maori did well in trade at the end of the nineteenth century. We even had our own trade flag, which is now used by the P&O Shipping Company. It belonged to us and I think someone sold it. You know, the Pakeha never stole anything—I mean, they insist that they never stole anything from us. They brought in new amendments, like they tried to take Rotorua, but they never stole it. What they did is what they are doing now. Maori are still accepting low wages. Maori still accept that they are the shovel hands. There was no difference back then. Pakeha come in, give you a couple of candy bars for your children and some rifles, and I suppose that was considered enough payment for a few acres of land. There is no way that they stole it! Our people accepted it. We were ignorant of Pakeha ways, we were less educated, and we found out that we got ripped off. Being less educated in terms of Pakeha ways, I bet you that most Maori did not even know what a crown was. Our chiefs talked in *koreros* [meetings]— that was our *mana*.

I once expressed my views to a Pakeha about what they had done over the years. He replied, "Well, Maori accepted and that is it." I said, "Oh, but you should read it properly. You were supposed to give us the land back, it was expected, and that is the other side of the coin. Did Maori fully understand that the land would be lost forever?" He replied, "Oh yes, they had interpreters there." I asked, "Who were those interpreters?" He answered, "Oh, Governor Grey's own right-hand man was an interpreter, he had learned Maori." I said, "I still have to come to terms with the English language and I feel that I am pretty incompetent with it, so how much did that interpreter know?" His interpretation of what was said back to the Maori and then back to Governor Grey is two different streets!

Do you view work as providing you with a place in society and a pattern for life? Does it provide you with a structure for your day?

If I did not work I would be flushed from European society, but I can still rely upon survival within the *whanau* structure, where we can be put to work. It is like this, one is working for a reward, one is working to survive. But if one was put to the survival test, you would find a huge swing in attitude towards an upbringing where you were taught to rely on your own resources. If I had no job and I was given a bit of land, I could work the land and survive. That is my Maori side. In the European world I need to have a job for survival. The incentive to get off welfare has gone for quite a lot of Maori, but these people have become street-smart. They use this skill as a small victory to beat the European system. Why should you go to work if you could stay home to look after your family?

In the Pakeha community such practice is frowned upon. How does the Maori world regard it?

In the Maori way of thinking you are with the people you want to be with—in other words, your children—and you are getting paid for it. So in Maori opinion you are doing the right thing, you are looking after your children.

Are you saying that the family in your community takes centre place in importance and where the money comes from is a secondary concern?

No, the family is not humiliated by you being out of a job. Nevertheless, if you are on the benefit and your father held a position for twenty-five years and you and other members of the family are not doing as well, people might start asking questions: "Hey, how about you boys, your dad held a job for a long time." But they are quick with their praises when your family is doing well too. So the Maori concept of how unemployment affects a Maori depends on the individual's state of mind, which determines how he views the situation himself. Maori do not think, "Gee, I am out of a job, I have to look for something else or my life is not worth living." It is not like that. However, someone may offer you a few days' work here and there—the job may turn into a full-time one, but the person will not surrender the benefit for another month or two. But if he gets caught he loses his benefit. His work performance may suffer because his morale does, and all of a sudden he is back in situation one, where he is back on the benefit. But now he has to pay back twenty dollars a week to WINZ because of his deceitful action in the past. And so he pushes himself more backward. This is how Maori work—I am talking from experience. I have been there, I have been the one being deceitful and I have had things repossessed too. This is real-life stuff.

What constitutes the difference between the city-bound Maori and those who are still living in rural areas?

Nothing. They [the government] just want to separate us. They now have someone with a university degree saying, "Look, we come in and help you sort out what the government is saying." The Nga Puhi tribe is an example. Their elders are not educated. Doug Graham [a member of parliament] says, "You urban Maori, you get out, I want to deal with these old people. We give you trinkets, some lollies, and then you will say that you are sorry and you will have no problems with us anymore."

These Maori chiefs act with their hearts. They don't know what the written facts are and so they allow us to be split apart. Our *kaumatua* know we cannot push them. *Educated potatoes* they call us: brown on the outside, white on the inside. We cannot convince them to the contrary. The rural *kaumatua* don't want a Maori boy who has not been back home to keep his home fires burning to tell them things. That makes you *kootaha*. The government is aware of this situation and, for that reason, wants to keep urban and rural Maori apart. *Kotahitanga* means that we must progress together in units—that is my family's concept. And to get proper units in Maoridom, you must eat together, share a job together, and you must sleep together on the *marae* as one.

What happens when someone says that he does not care about the family any longer because he has a job, a house, and the like?

It happens all the time, but such things do not fit in our structure. We all say, "What goes around comes around." Life is a big circle—there are no sanctions for that type of thing. If that person comes back to the *marae*, he will find that if he had once been a head carver, he would now be the boy cleaning up. [Wood carving is a prestigious skill.] Thus, status as far as work goes drops. An important job goes down to a menial task, that is all. But we will take care of him or her too—they will still be fed. Their situation will not affect the rest of the family. A black sheep is always welcomed back.

As for me, I have stayed close to my roots and I can go for advice to certain of my elders. If I want to talk about finances I go to my *wairu*, my spiritual leaders. I, too, have nephews and nieces who come to me and ask about schooling because

I have a reputation of being able to help them. The path that my own children will choose is theirs—I have given them Maori and Pakeha options. I cannot remove the Pakeha from their world and the Pakeha cannot remove us! That is the end of the story!

* * *

This interview with Adam discloses his ideational system, in which the concept of work has been shaped by the culture and traditions of a people who, despite their gradual migration into New Zealand suburbia, have retained their distinct identity as Maori, the *tanga whenua* (people of the land). Attending the Mormon Church College in Hamilton, New Zealand, sharpened Adam's awareness of the differences in the Pakeha and Maori ways of being while allowing him to observe the benefits of adhering to some of the market ideals and philosophies of mainstream society.

At the onset of the interview, Adam maintained his distance and appeared careful not to reveal too much of his Maori ways before me, a Pakeha woman. But as the conversation progressed he became aware that his Maori and my Mormon ways shared some common ground. He also realized that my lengthy stay in New Zealand had familiarized me with sufficient Maoritanga to understand his point of view. At that point, he allowed himself to express his Maori thoughts and feelings in terms understood by both of us.

In the early part of the interview, Adam discussed his ambitions for his own working life and those of his children, which covered the education and training needed to achieve a certain standard of living and to maximize the benefits of holding a steady job. Nevertheless, these thoughts were still expressed in the Maori context of expectations, which always included the elders of his *hapu* and considerations of *whanau* and other Maori. His expectations were always set in the traditional context of past and present, as expressed through the phrase *keeping one's paths mowed*, meaning to keep the way back to the village open and well-trodden.

The interview suggests that prior to the arrival of the Europeans, Maori social institutions were consistent, as Adam illustrated with the triangle he drew. Adam insisted that the Europeans turned their world upside down by placing the triangle and all its structures, institutions, values, and beliefs on its head, where it teeters precariously, propped up by means that have spelled disaster for Maori. God and traditional leadership have been rendered insignificant, with their *mana* reduced in significance by the Pakeha regime.

To Adam the real danger of alienation from his roots lies in climbing to success within the Pakeha structure without keeping the way open to the village and the *marae*. A Maori in that situation finds himself quickly in no man's land, not really belonging to either world. As the members of one's *hapu* and *whanau* could be very helpful in aiding one's plans for the future, so could they hold back and keep down someone who tried to ignore the village rules. Adam explained that if Maori people want to get ahead, they pull others up with them rather than taking opportunities on their own. In the contemplation of options, expectations, and ambitions in working life, the emphasis is always on the *whanau*, the company of others, in contrast to Westerners, who have individual ambitions and prepare for participation in the labour market from an early age.

During the interview, Adam often referred to the *marae*, a Maori gathering place where food is communally consumed and where people sleep together. Understanding this aspect of Maori communal life is significant if one is keen to understand the principal of *awhi mai te whanau*, to hug or embrace your family.

The interaction between the present and the past provides Maori with a perspective of their world, which Adam illustrated with his story about the decision making of the Nga Puhi chief who needed to confer with his god to make the right decision for his people. It clearly illustrates the inter-connection of the esoteric and the practical in the Maori world, which is notably at variance with Western ways of thinking. The holistic aspect of Maori thought and action is expressed in their ideas about work and the need to work together in groups in which people can see and touch each other, and is further proof that the individualistic actions and ideas of the Pakeha contrast significantly with the all-encompassing objective of the *whanau* system.

The principle of being streetwise offers unemployed Maori people a source of income, even if it is regarded as unacceptable by Pakeha standards. Being streetwise needs to be viewed in the context of Maori taking care of the many obligations that they have toward the *whanau* and the *hapu*. These obligations need to be met, it seems, at all costs, re-gardless of the source of finances, as long as the source does not involve theft or other criminal behaviour, which could harm the *mana* of a group as a whole.

According to Adam, the loss of one's job does not incur feelings of despair to the extent that non-Maori workers may experience, unless the individual has been discharged dis-honourably through certain actions on his part. There ap-pears to be no loss of *mana*, nor is there a need to feel less acceptable or less part of communal life.

Adam also referred to the way in which Maori teach their young, which is visual and very practical. Adam has noted that Pakeha and Maori ideational systems will never con-verge, as they have, for him, continuously manifested a run-ning parallel.

The next chapter portrays the experiences of two Maori women who were brought up in a rural area in the traditional Maori way and migrated to the city

Chapter 6
Rural and Urban Differences

The next four participants are two women in their fifties and two younger men in their early forties: Mauri and David at the Trust Village, and Jane and Peta in Brisbane. I interviewed them separately. My interviews with them illuminated important ways of thinking and being in Maori village life and work, for both children and adults. All four interviewees had moved from rural settings to urban areas, and their experiences in the Pakeha world had provided them with certain perceptions about social life in mainstream New Zealand society.

Mauri stated that she was in her middle fifties and came from a Maori, Norwegian, and Swedish background. In early childhood, she lived in a Maori setting in the care of her great-grandparents, who taught her the basics of survival, which included fetching water from the well, serving the members and elders of the *whanau*, and the value of work in general. All Maori children had responsibilities such as homemaking, economic skills, and repairing fishing nets. Mauri had received some years of formal schooling in rural towns. By the time she was twelve years old, Mauri left school to seek employment in the Pakeha world, as her great-grandparents had passed away and there was no one else to take care of her in the village. Mauri insisted that early childhood training had contributed to her ability to adapt to new conditions in her life. She commented that if one had to live without electricity, one needed to learn to gather driftwood to start a fire. "If you don't have a fire, you are not able to boil water, cook food, or keep yourself warm."

Mauri's Story

Do you consider having a job and earning money to be for the benefit of the family?

We have to have money today, there is no denying that, but it is the goals that signify the difference. Money is a big part of life, but if anything happened to the New Zealand economy, I would have no problem gathering seafood, growing my own vegetables, and preparing and preserving food. Money is essential, but it does not govern all aspects of life. If I had to take care of someone who is ill, I would not expect to be paid for my efforts. If you do not take opportunities to learn, you will never know. I was taught survival skills in my village and I made good use of them.

Who taught you these skills? Were they members of your whanau?

Wait, I have the information, I shall show you. [Mauri produced some documents with pictures on them.] My great-grandmother was the descendant of Pomare, an important chief, and my great-grandfather's line is from Te Whiti [the chief in the Taranaki area who initiated passive resistance against further sales of Maori land in the 1860s]. They were my teachers, as they provided me with basic skill training when I was very little. They taught me about safety, how to read the winds and the ocean, when to plant crops, how to bake bread, and how to preserve. I was taught in Maori by my great-grandparents, and I learned from them to choose words that are powerful. Besides that, they taught me to do whatever I did effectively and with skill, as it would save me a lot of hard work and wasted energy in the end. They were very prayerful and said prayers before they went out and before they prepared their garden—they gave me my spiritual foundation. They also taught me always to put family first. My great-grandfather used to look after people—he delivered babies in the village. He was a jack-of-all-trades, but he was a master of some. He prepared medicinal potions and oils and things like that. He knew all plants in the bush and he showed me which parts of plants were used for certain things.

Was he a tohunga *[priest]?* [Mauri had been guarded in her responses to my questions up to this point. She did not volunteer much detail, but seemed to be trying to impress me with things that she thought I liked and ought to hear.]

Yes, he was a *tohunga*—you know about these things? I did not want to mention anything about it. Yes, my great-grandmother comes from such a lineage too. It is very powerful knowledge. Some things I do not talk about to anybody because they were given me for my protection. My great-grandmother used to chant Maori songs to me about the moon and the stars and explained to me why we were on earth. She was well known for her strength in the district. She worked all her life in the gardens, in the village—she was wonderful. She could not read or write but her strength lay in what she knew.

* * *

Mauri continued to explain her experiences with *tohunga*, who are the receptacles of spiritual knowledge, natural medicines, and things that are to be regarded as *tapu*. She confided to me that *tohunga* are involved with spiritual things because they understand them, as they have been given special gifts. Her great-grandfather's area of expertise was concerned with helping women to give birth, giving people direction and guidance, and taking care of them when they were sick. Because Mauri's great-grandfather's forebears were European through his father's line, he did not own Maori land, although his European side did procure sufficient land holdings. Mauri commented that every bit of land owned by the Pakeha side of her great-grandfather's family had been acquired through theft. She argued this point by saying that she had documents in her possession that showed that the family had deeds to the land although they had not bought it.

Mauri further explained that her great-grandfather was born on the land of his pioneer forebears, but that none of his Maori descendants had ever gone there to live, as they considered it desecrated since it had been bought with alcohol and trinkets. She admitted that it was rich and productive land near an ocean full of all kinds of seafood. There was even a *whare wananga* (house of learning) on that land. The institution of *whare wananga* conveys that Maori see their world from a spiritual perspective and that they learn to appreciate and cherish their surroundings through its teachings.

As a child, Mauri became aware of the difference in colour between her great-grandfather and other men in the village. She was told by the men that the problems and land conflicts between Maori and Pakeha did not rest with the former, but were the result of the fact that the Europeans could not survive in their own country and had come to New Zealand to get hold of the land at all cost. According to Mauri, they used the term *tauiwi* (stranger) when they referred to the colonizers, rather than the more familiar phrase Pakeha.

Your feelings about work, your beliefs and values, do you feel that other Maori share them?

Of course they don't think the way that I do. If they have not had the same background as I have had, they will not begin to understand. I support people who look after their own families to the best of their ability. There are a lot of Maori out there who do good things. They are not even acknowledged or recognized because the work they do is regarded as voluntary or community work and is, therefore, unrewarded in monetary terms. Much of these skills have been fostered in the home, unrecognized by mainstream society as worthy to be mentioned as work in the workforce. I find that there is a level of abuse in this. I feel that all work should be acknowledged—work is work no matter what one does.

Instead of all the spiritual things being the foundation, Maoridom has been exposed to a lot of things that are of very little value in our lives. Maori have been caught in a trap of control. My people have always had a spiritual foundation, but things have been turned around today. Even the land became the foundation instead of the spirit, or the *atua*, meaning God.

Nowadays the brain tells the spirit where one's foundation is. When you get further down the track you find that flesh controls the spirit. Instead of the family being the strength and responsibility of what happens in the home, society takes over the family. With the old way we could handle what came our way, but they have turned the whole structure upside down. That is the trap that we find ourselves in now, and we don't know how to address it. People have disregarded their foundations—whether we speak of Maori or Pakeha, it is all the same. No matter how they try to turn things around again, they cannot fix it. All these poor people are told now to go and find a job. They need to clean up their acts and stop boasting about their positions and their jobs. Maori people are quite happy to stay at home and to take care of their children properly. A mother must stand at the door waiting for children to come home from school. But that has now changed—presently, they are told that they have to work too. And that is why I ask: what is their idea of work, what is it for? Why do a father and a mother both have to work seven days a week? Does the next generation have to bring up itself? No matter what type of work people perform, they should be paid for it, whether it is visiting or helping in schools, or the like. This is how I feel about it, and for Maori it has always been a hard struggle to understand all of it.

Jane's Story

Jane moved from New Zealand to Brisbane some years ago. She commenced her story by recounting her childhood in the rural areas of the southeast side of the North Island. Although her father was Pakeha, she spent her early childhood in a typical Maori setting where Maori was spoken.

Can you tell me something about your childhood?

Childhood play was unknown. Children worked and shared games and laughter as they carried out their duties. People shared tools and horses to get the fields ploughed, as working in the fields was a common affair. The children had the task of taking care of the horses—they weeded after school and did other chores. Children were kept occupied in their spare time—there was no time to get bored. The horses were quite big, but we sat on them and afterwards headed for the creek to wash them. If somebody had mentioned "play" to me, I would not have been able to recognise that we engaged in any. It was a learning time, which was always associated with work. My mother had gone to the city to work, and that meant that we children were instructed by the old people, who taught us about what was expected of us as they brought us up. That is why we all had to help out and do the work. It was mainly to produce food and engage in other activities for survival.

Why was your mother's generation sent to the cities to work at the time?

It was to earn money, as there was nothing in the villages. Most people were very poor. Perhaps we were slightly better off than most, but my grandparents shared with others in the *hapu* and other families in the village. There were certain seasons for certain produce, such as blackberries, of which we made jam and which we traded at the Red Cross for clothing in the 1950s.

Migration to the towns and cities began in the 1950s. My mother came back to the village from time to time, wearing nice clothes and shoes, showing off all the things she was able to buy in the city. She also brought home cans of oil for the gas stove. We still washed in the creek.

Children were taught not to eat anything that was green on the trees because it was *tapu*. The ruling applied to all the people. Girls and women were not allowed to work in the gardens when they had their periods. They were not allowed to touch the food. They could prepare it, but they were forbidden to pull it out of the ground. As long as it was cooked, it was all right, and as long as it had come away from the land. They were not to collect it out of the garden to bring it in.

How difficult was it for you to move from the land to the city? Was the transition easy?

When we migrated to the city, I thought at first that it would be wonderful. One of the remarkable things was the change in diet that we experienced, as it was different from living off the produce of the land. Everything was already cleaned and prepared—in other words, the meat, chicken, and fish were bought ready to be cooked. In the village we only ate chicken on special occasions, or pigeons. There was a *tapu* put on various foodstuffs during certain seasons in the village, which meant that you were not allowed to partake of them. The *tapu* was put on purely to conserve these food and other consumer goods, as in the village there never was that much. The difference between village life and city life was that the workers, the men, would eat first, and that the children were to wait their turn. This was to ensure that the men were fed well first after a hard day's work. It took me many years to come to terms with the new practice of feeding the children last, as there were many children in the household.

On the *marae* the children were mostly allowed to do as they pleased, but in the city they had to get used to the European way of doing things. We children were allowed to be children on the *marae*. In the village we were taught by our great-uncle and aunt; in the city we were taken care of by our parents. On the *marae* we were aware of the status that the various members of the family held in their ranking of eldest down to the youngest. The youngest sibling served the eldest, as he was the dominant person and had to be obeyed by the youngest, who had to drop everything to obey the call. Work to Maori means giving to and sharing with of what one has with others.

I moved to Ponsonby in the Auckland area with my family and was told that I had to attend the local school in order to

be able to get a job later in life. But from the start I was made
to understand that I was different from the Pakeha children
at school. I learned that one of the girls at my school was
giving a party one afternoon, and when I turned up at the
house of the girl, I was turned away with the message that
I had not been invited and that Maori were not welcome.
I had never before considered that parties and other social
gatherings might be exclusive affairs rather than the drop-in
versions I had been used to in the village. I also realized that
at school things were different for Maori children, as I had
to learn more in order to overcome the cultural differences
in obtaining the knowledge. The first restriction comprised
the exclusion of the use of the Maori language at school. I
could no longer speak in Maori with other Maori children at
school, a fact that was enforced with caning and the use of
the strap for those who disobeyed this rule. The consequence
for Maori children was that we were severely disadvantaged
in the school system because we were not able to express
ourselves in our own language, being severely punished if
we did, and not able to cope with an entirely different system and environment and an overall hostile social climate,
which put up social barriers that had the function of keeping
us, who were different, out.

*Jane continued her story by explaining the role of men
and women in Maori ceremonies and rituals. These ceremonies continued in the urban maraes.*

Upon entering a *marae*, all the people gather outside the
gate, where they have to wait for a woman to call *karanga*,
or ceremonial call. The men have great respect for this
ceremony because one cannot gain entrance to the *marae*
without it. It also sets up the atmosphere for the *hui* [social
gathering], or the *tangi* [funeral rites]. Female dominance
is apparent on such an occasion—the role is generally ful-
filled by the *kuias* [old women]. If there is no *karanga*, the
man on the *marae* calls out and inquires who the visitors are.
Traditionally, permission to enter the *marae* came from the
kaumaatua [elders]. You did not ask too many questions or

question certain rules—everybody had their place. Women worked and organized things in the kitchen; the men busied themselves with the *hangi* [in-ground oven]. The women gathered; the men hunted and worked in the plantations. There was a strict division of roles, which did not hint at the domination of men in any way. My mother always knew her place on the *marae*, and that is what my English stepfather could not understand. Because she was the youngest in her family, she just followed her sisters and half-brothers because they were her elders. Every time they went back to the *marae*, she would work in the kitchen. There are many *hapus* in a family who share a *marae*. Women marry out and to the *marae* of their husbands. Maori women have rights to land, even after they are married, but the land remains the property of the *hapu*. Her children have access to that land, but not her husband.

Can you tell me something about the work organization of the Maori in the towns?

Lots of Maori worked in the freezing works in Hastings, the local city on the east coast. It became the big *marae* because families worked together. You knew everybody, and people continued their relationships even outside work. They played together—they were like a family, just like a *hapu*. When the freezing works closed down, it was a terrible thing for the Maoris, like the termination of a family. Back home in the village, the *whanau* would engage in pig hunting from time to time, and the job of the children was to chase the pigs with the dogs. It was the job of the men to prepare the pig meat and put it in the *hangi* to be cooked. We lead busy and active lives. Whether on the land or in the city, it is the same.

Peta's Account

Peta is a Maori man who lives in Brisbane and is married to a Pakeha woman who was born in New Zealand. Peta was also brought up in a rural setting, where he attended school and where most of his friends were Maori and from the same background. He explained that as a Maori boy he never wanted to excel in anything or develop his potential, although his teachers at school encouraged him by saying that he could do much better and could go to university later in life. But the desire was not there. Peta underscored his attitude by explaining that all the Maori men in his district had worked in the freezing works for generations, and that the ambition to do better was not part of their growing-up.

You went to school and then to the freezing works, where you worked together with members of your *whanau* and *hapu* and other *hapus*. It was the same for your schoolmates. Our goals and objectives were different, as we were used to doing everything in the group. Family was more important than the pursuit of a career.

What made you decide to move to Brisbane?

I had married a Pakeha girl who experienced discrimination in a reversed order of what the Maori generally experience in non-Maori settings. She was subjected to verbal abuse when the villagers picked up their dole checks when she worked at the New Zealand Post Office. It resulted in her demands that we move away from the Maori surroundings and settle in the city, where she would feel more comfortable in her own environment. I realised that having married a non-Maori, I would have to consider her demands, although Maori decisions are customarily made in the group. Husbands consult with the family, but not with their wives, who as a rule never question the decisions that are made. There was one other consideration, namely, my wife and I are members of the Church of Jesus Christ of Latter-day Saints, which teaches that it is not wrong to question decisions as husbands and wives make them together and between themselves alone. At the same time, however, I know that achievement on my part would have been more conducive to success, but I had not been encouraged to aspire to greater heights in my environment.

I was brought up in the country and so were my parents. We lived close to a *marae*. There was only one shop in the district, and everyone I associated with in our area on the east coast of the North Island was Maori and stayed and worked in that environment. I never saw white people just walking around until I went to Hastings, the nearest city. I belonged to the Ngati Kahununu Tribe. Some farmers in the district were white and they hired Maori workers. Maori ran farms too that had been handed down to them from generation to generation. Work was a shared thing as well as an obligation. Many Maori were engaged in sheep shearing, which they did on the farms, but my parents had their own land that was left to them by the family. Young Maori were taught that it was the tradition of the family to work for the family as opposed to just getting things for private use. Working is the thing to do. My dad started work when he was in grade six or seven.

From a Maori point of view, what do you consider to be work? Is it the paid job or something else?

Dad worked on the family farm but did not get paid for it. You worked because you needed to survive. When he married, he left the farm and stayed in the rural areas but went to the city to work. We were taught to work from a very young age by having to do odd jobs. In the Maori world, work is a shared opportunity for survival, not to obtain riches. Our parents taught that we had to share with those who had not. It was not our goal to get rich, but to help other people in the community. That was what motivated my parents to work, to survive, to support the family and survive together as a people. The notion of Pakeha work, that you have to get ahead, is not bad, but Maori people on the whole are not too interested in that concept, although there are exceptions on the rule, especially in the last twenty-two years.

The Maori population in the prisons in New Zealand is quite large. What could be the reason for this?

Because of Pakeha pressure in the urban areas, many of the Maori people find that they cannot live their culture in that setting, nor can they cope with Pakeha demands on their "commitment to work" effort. It is frustrating. You get used to breaking the rules because they are not your rules anyway.

Can you tell me something about the experience of Maori in education?

In the Maori world, a child's first teachings occurred in the home, usually through the elders in the *whanau*. When we started school, our teachers were Maori and so were most of the children. This situation lasted until we reached grade three or four. But we soon had to go to school in the city, where we were caned for speaking Maori with our friends. It resulted in the feeling of loss in the city and the feeling of not belonging. The big difference was that there was such an emphasis on doing your best to excel in school, whereas in the Maori school situation that had not been important. There were certain activities in Maoridom that had prestige attached to them, one of which was that of the Maori carver, which was a very prestigious art and skill. Dad was a master carver. He taught us boys to carve.

We children learned to observe to laws of *tikanga* when we went to the *marae*—it meant that we needed to do what the grown-ups told us to do, although as children we really did not do very much on the *marae*. For children, work was play. Like my dad, we left school early to help the family. Formal education was not important, but work was. My brother wanted to be a carver—that was his education. He trained under a master carver and is now one of only three carvers left in New Zealand.

How did the law of tapu fit into work and the division of labour?

The men always prepared the *hangi* and worked together because they are *tapu*. The women had separate duties inside, being *noa*. Women never did men's work, nor did men do the work of women. The division of labour is just that: outside versus inside, *tapu* versus *noa*.

Maori women say that Maori men are too slow and that is the reason that Maori women forge ahead now and make decision in the urban areas.

That is true, men don't like to push forward. They were never encouraged to excel academically or to push forward. We were brought up that men gave the orders, that they were in control in certain areas and women took care of other things. It is very hard when in the Pakeha world a woman gives orders to men. Everything is so mixed up, and that gets us confused. When a man wandered into the sphere of activity of the women, they used to say to him, "You go where the men are, this is where we women work." Women hanging around the men were also sent away. Women have to do their tasks—they have their own sphere and place. We understood those things because they are natural to us, that is our culture. When a meetinghouse is being built, the women must stay outside and do the mat weaving there. They are not allowed within the structure until it is completed.

Maori are easygoing, they are not in a rush to get anywhere. They have no long-term goals. It is different in Brisbane, where everyone is rushing around trying to accumulate wealth or work for their future. Something to get used to. I just worked for what I needed, and that was it. In your culture you have to live up to the demands your culture places on you and you do what you can. We Maori take our time in doing things. For the Pakeha it is crucial to excel academically for the survival in their world of work. Maori do not care about that. We do not place such importance on it, which is sad in a way because in the city, today, you have to work harder when you don't have any qualifications. In today's world, you have to obtain qualifications at an academic level just to provide for your family. My parents did not push education onto us, and that attitude was instilled in us. Now we see how important it is to try to encourage our children to do well in school.

The Views of David at the Waipareira Trust

David is a young man who came from a tribe in the far north of the North Island and whose area of work at the Waipareira Trust Village was one of considerable responsibility. It had been difficult to get a hold of him, but once we were seated in his office and the interview began, he relaxed and was quite eager to explain his point of view.

Pakeha invariably comment that Maori drain the nation's funds for their projects, especially when these are seen to be failing.

Pakeha argue that Maori get extensive funding for their projects, but the truth is that such funding comes from Maori land trusts. There may be an imbalance in the moneys available to Maori, but these are to address a bigger imbalance in society where the Maori people are concerned. Maori have a much harder time to catch up in the Pakeha society, whereas Pakeha children achieve in their own system. In Maori society, it was the chiefs and the *kaumaatua* [elders] who were teaching the young people on the *marae*.

There are two key points to be considered here. A lot of *kaumaatua* harbour bitterness, anger, and resentment because they have not been able to mobilize people into action. Years of fighting for what they want and finally getting it come to nothing, because they have become so impatient and fail to sit down to plan things properly. That is why funds dwindle and mistakes are made. They do not sit down and plan the next step. For most Maori there is no next step—they fight and fight to get what is rightfully theirs, and when they finally get what they want, there is no plan to be implemented for proper use to benefit the people. You do have a lot of chiefs who are at the helm but who are not really skilful enough, or do not have the skills or the knowledge to utilize the funds.

Maori knowledge of the Pakeha political system has only evolved and developed in the last one hundred years or more. Pakeha have used their political system and the knowledge to operate it for hundreds of years. For Maori it is something relatively new. For Maori it is different because they come from a different cultural background.

Can you explain a little bit more about the Maori person and how he or she feels about today's conditions?

Tuakiritangata, which means "beyond the skin," or "metaphysical." Elements that are beyond the physical. There are about nine or ten elements that make up a Maori person, of which I will name three: *Pmanawa*, inherited traits, or quirks, things that you were born with, as opposed to *mana*, which is bestowed, not inherited. People can also take away *mana*. Other people need to bestow it on you. *Connection* between yourself and your ancestors on the *marae* is depicted through the structure of the meetinghouse. That is how we Maori still see the world and our position in it.

Maori women are said to be taking the lead, according to one woman.

She is right, Maori women are taking the lead in mainstream society today. For Maori men it is a lot more difficult than for Maori women. There are a lot of things that hold Maori men back, whereas Maori women can forge ahead. Within their own perceptions, they can do that because they have a lot more freedom to do so. For Maori men there are the issues of their *mana*. Sometimes working in a non-Maori environment is a lot more difficult for the men because there are things that they cannot express or announce. There are the issues of men being *tapu* and women being *noa*. Traditionally Maori men occupied specific roles in our own society, which they no longer have, and that is why they hold back. We see that a lot in Maori men who are registered as unemployed. It is a very embarrassing and shameful position for them, although they contribute to the welfare of their families in a number of other ways in unpaid work. It is a very difficult thing for a Maori man to be interviewed at WINZ by a woman, who is clearly in a position of authority over him in that situation. It is the principle of *mana* versus *noa* that operates here.

So, which system puts the negative label or stigma on the unemployed Maori person, the Pakeha or Maori?

It is a Pakeha stigma. Being unemployed is regarded as an antisocial thing that happens when you lose your income from paid work and are unable to provide for your own means of support. But for Maori, work may not necessarily be counted in terms of dollars and cents. One still contributes, although this type of work is not valued in the Pakeha world. When a person becomes unemployed, he or she is seen as a negative statistic in mainstream society, and they talk about Maori men being disadvantaged in the labour market. But a lot of it has to do with *mana* and *tapu*—everything comes back to that. A lot of Maori do not realize that and wonder why they are not moving or forging ahead, but there are all these problems there, and they do not realize that there are these issues that they need to look at.

Do you find that Maori often get offended in a non-Maori environment because of the tapu *issues?*

Yes, issues of the head and feet, and dead bodies. Washing your hair in a sink in which dishes are washed—the head is *tapu*. Stepping over a dead body, especially when it belongs to a man, is *tapu*. Cutting hair at a hairdresser's, the hair is left there—it has to be put in a bag and buried on the land or in the garden. Sitting on a dinner table on which food is served is also not allowed. For Maori that is very offensive. The Waipareira Village is a different environment because it is Maori. Maori men are a lot more relaxed and happy here because a lot of the barriers that they would encounter in a non-Maori situation are eliminated. Some of these issues are gender-based differences. You have to have Maori men working with Maori men because of the traditional separation between the sexes, or the division of labour. In the urban centres, Maori men tend to get aggressive with women because they are thrown together more often, which creates problems, especially in the domestic sphere. Maori women work better with other women too. For instance, if WINZ makes an appointment with a Maori and he does not turn up for his appointment and even fails to attend the next interview, his benefit would be cut off. Such confrontation represents a gross insult to a Maori man. Just to sit across the table and to have to explain himself to someone who is not Maori in order to have his benefit restored is regarded as degrading for a Maori, especially if the interviewer happens to be a Pakeha woman. In Pakeha culture, it is quite appropriate for the interviewer to insist on knowing the reason for someone not keeping a previous appointment, but for a Maori it is not. Such cultural differences need to be taken into account. The same thing happens when they talk about equal opportunity. It is the Pakeha who decides, "This is important for you." Maori become suspicious and resist, although it may actually benefit Maori. Emphasis on acquisition of wealth is still not an important issue for Maori. It is still an irrelevant matter for the individual, unless it benefits the whole family.

When do Maori consider themselves to be poor?

The definition of poverty for Maori is not perceived in the material sense. A Maori would be poor if he had no contact with family or relatives. You can be flat broke with no money at all, but you have your family around you and you are rich. The challenge for Maori is to do what they can do for Maori, something that benefits Maori as a whole. *Maori tinorangatiratanga* [self-determination] is what Maori are saying— "This is where we want to go." In terms of the treaty, it is a matter of the Crown recognizing this and supporting it rather than saying how Maori should go or telling them what they should do. The Crown should, instead, stand back and ask, "Where do you want to go, Maori? Mobilize yourselves, get moving, we back you up." Maori may decide that they do not want to be part of the world scene. They may take an alternative approach and take the opposite view. Rather than expanding, they might come back into themselves and regrow. They may decide, "We as a people are not ready to put ourselves on the world map yet." We Maori need to redefine ourselves and make sure that every

Maori is in the same playing field. A lot of Maori know that they are Maori, but some don't know who they are.

Maori need to withdraw into themselves again to strengthen themselves. When they decide to take a bold step forward, they take it as a people. Then they can tell the world who they are as a people. If Pakeha would support Maori initiatives, they would be alongside as well. The relationship between Maori and non-Maori in this country has not been sorted out yet. The concern for Maori is always the danger that they will fade away as a people if they are not careful, if they don't watch out. There are a lot of Maori movements around the country, but Maori need to step forward as a people, united in their objectives. It is difficult for Maori to move outside their *iwi* or *hapu* boundaries. In traditional times, you only did so to fight with another tribe down the line. When you break down the traditional structure of your own *rangatira* [chiefs] and your *hapu* to go outside your boundaries, that is a difficult thing to do. But in today's world, we are scattered to the four winds. It is a matter of collecting them all together.

Now we have that—we have a very strong, mobilized body of Maori looking at educational scholarships. We are looking at promoting within the family the idea of people who can study medicine, some who move into the fields of science and information technology. It has only just started over the last few years, but we have the mix right. Now, that is how we as a people are going to determine what we want. The idea of having lawyers, doctors, physicists, and the like is to contribute back to the family again. That is where we are at, at present. It is not about money. It comprises the need of getting the people back in again and educating them. We are part of a bigger *whanau* of five thousand. We put our resources in there, expanding all the time. We'll have *iwi* supporting *iwi*. In time, we may have non-Maori, such as the Pacific Islanders, joining us in the movement.

* * *

The interviews with my four participants in this chapter portray how profoundly their ideational systems about work vary from those of their Pakeha counterparts. The first three participants were born and spent their childhoods in rural areas, being raised and taught by the elders of the *whanaus* while their parents were away at work in the local towns. David left for the city at an early age. However, he told me that he was frequently in touch with his village and that the members of his *whanau* came together regularly on his *marae* to be instructed by his uncle, who was a chief. The childhood transition from village to city was painful for my participants, who reported suffering and disorientation. Not only did they have to adjust to a Pakeha school system, which demanded speedy integration, but they also had to negotiate proscription against the use of the Maori language on school grounds.

The interviews with these four participants provided valuable information about the division of labour in Maori society, which was suggested as a key factor in the reluctance of Maori men to assert themselves in the labour market via higher skill training. The participants demonstrated how the principles of *mana*, *tapu*, and *noa* continue to be prominent in their ideational systems about work, and that these beliefs and their associated practices are reasons why Pakehas represent Maori ways of thinking as insurmountable obstacles to Pakeha-defined success. The participants described how Maori work and live in groupings of extended family members and how, when it became necessary for men and women to seek work in the local towns in the freezing works or road works, they opted for those jobs because it meant that members of a *whanau* could work together, see and touch each other, and be embraced by the group. Indeed, David explained that the structure of the meetinghouse on the *marae* represents an ancestor in whose bosom the members of the tribe meet together.

David has shown that Maori are able to "get ahead," but their success will be on their own terms as a people, with their culture, language, and institutions intact. The paths that they will take may be parallel to those of the Pakeha, but may also be in an opposite direction. Pakeha efforts to improve the living standard of Maori may not fully succeed on Pakeha terms because of the collective nature of Maori social and economic ideational systems. Viewed from this perspective, it becomes clear that the Maori people are disadvantaged in the labour market and education system, which became all too apparent when the freezing works in many parts of the North Island were closed down.

David explained Maori enterprise in mainstream society from a Maori point of view, describing a Maori setting in which traditional practices are observed in order to retain a strong sense of *whanau*. He accentuated the opposition between *tapu* and *noa,* noting how Maori men hang back in the labour market while women take the lead in taking up Maori causes in welfare leagues that cater to their own people.

The participants also described how many Pakeha practices are inherently offensive to Maori people, and that such cultural differences can represent an obstacle to the assimilation of Maori people into mainstream society. The disparity between the Pakeha and Maori concepts of poverty shows how two different perceptions about work and life have created directly opposed systems of thought. For the former, poverty means a state of deprivation, while for many Maori people, a lack of funds is not traumatising if they are in the company of their family members.

The next chapter deals with the experiences of two *kaumaatua* (Maori elders): a manager of a Maori skills training school, and an employee of a New Zealand government department.

Chapter 7
Maori Perceptions of Sociocultural Change

The first interview was conducted in the home of Aporo, a Maori elder, who had invited Matiu, another elder, to take part in its proceedings, and who soon took the lead in the interview. These two participants were elderly and knowledgeable about Maori ways and history. Both had started their lives in rural areas and had moved to the Auckland suburbs as adults. Sadly, Aporo passed away two years after the interview took place. Matiu was well known as a protestor against the injustices sustained by his people in Pakeha society.

Tom, a third interviewee, was raised in a rural area as the son of a chief and moved to Auckland as a young adult. He is the head of a school that trains Maori youth in building trade skills. Rangi was a member of the Maori Women's League and worked for the New Zealand Qualification Authority (NZQA), which audits Maori private training establishments, such as the one Tom managed, for their effectiveness in preparing Maori youth for the workforce.

Matiu and Aporo's Stories and Views

How meaningful is work to Maori people, Matiu?

We have a saying: "*Kamahi ko kai.*" When you work you eat, and without it you are nothing. In other words, if you do not work, you are lazy. The other thing Maori say is: "*Kohunokokaki paku,*" which means that you have a deep gullet and that you are putting your stomach before everything else. Again, it relates to work. My dad was taught when he was a boy that work is the noblest activity of all. Thus, when they say that Maori are lazy, that is rubbish. Our people are hard workers. Now, with the intervention of the Pakeha this became different. I am talking about the original work for our people on the *marae*, where the activities were. Work was consistent, being carried out on an everyday basis. People knew the value of work because we were well organized as a society. For instance, we had *kumara* plantations, we had Maori corn, potatoes, and *peruperu*, which is a type of potato. The people appreciated the value of work. Maori never worked for the kind of rewards that there are today. Everything that we did was centred in godly principles—that was true. The principles of faith, hope, and charity comprise the philosophy of work in the Maori context. For example, there was a *karakia* [prayer] attached to everything Maori did. If you chopped a tree, a *karakia* was offered. If you went fishing, another special *karakia* was given for that event. These are prayers, incantations—call them what you like. Can you see that? It was part and parcel of Maori philosophy, because everything that Maori did in relation to work and play or in religion involved spiritual consideration and input.

Other participants conveyed that the Maori concept of work does not imply just working for somebody, but work in relation to life and to the community as a whole. Do you see it that way too?

You got it! With family and extended family. On the other hand, a Maori who goes to work for somebody is loyal, and you find that if he works for a Pakeha, he would stay with that person. Maori are loyal in their relationships.

Matiu, is it true that when Maori are made redundant they are put to work on the marae, so whether they work in the context of the village or in the workforce, it really makes no difference to them?

Yes, one of the things is that Maori do not like working as individuals in the workplace, but prefer to be active in a collectivity. They are happier working as a unit, in cooperatives where they all work together. Not only in our own environment, but also in the Pakeha workforce. It is not only cooperative thinking, but such is the philosophy of Maori. If you help one, you are helping others as well.

Do Maori workers have ambition to be the boss or chief?

You may find that in Maori groups, even before the intervention of the white man, there are those who have the better ideas and who have higher positions than the others, even in today's world. But on the whole you will notice that Maori are collective, cooperative thinkers. They are not individuals in that sense because they like the whole tribe to succeed. You will find that if one member of the tribe gets ahead of the others, they want to pull him down. It is amazing that you should ask about work. In Maoridom it is a disgrace to sit at the table if you had not worked. If you sat at the table, the people around you knew straightaway that you did not deserve to sit there at all. "Where were you?" "Oh, I was down the road." "Well, you should have been here!"

The beauty of Maori society is that we lived in tribes. We did not know high hedges that outlined your section of land and property to define the place that belonged to you: "That is your fence and you stay behind your side of the fence." Maori lived with no fences at all. I remember that as a four-year-old child I had to get up at four in the morning to help strip the cows. We had to milk them, put the billy on, and spread the cream of the milk on our bread. We were taught how to work at a very early age. That is the beauty of most things in Maoridom. And so it was on the *marae*. We were taught all there was to know about its buildings, such as the *whare kai* [eating house], the *whare waananga* [house of learning], and the like. They taught your right from childhood to puberty and on from that. Once you approached manhood, or womanhood, you were separated from the opposite sex. The women had their own places where they were taught about women things, having babies and all that. The men would progress from one stage to another, too, until they finally achieved the desired levels in social skills and the arts. In short, all that men should and should not do, especially concerning their behaviour toward women.

* * *

Aporo and Matiu both went on to explain that in today's world, people receive mixed messages, and that because of brainwashing by the media and other agents, values are seriously undermined. In the traditional Maori setting, intensive learning about the environment, survival, and artistic endeavours took place as a matter of fact. Even the art of warfare and self-defence were part of the daily curriculum on the marae. Nevertheless, both elders agreed that training for the Maori people predominantly focused on spiritual and mental development.

How do Maori learn, and in what context does such learning take place?

Maori philosophy advocates helping each other: "*tatou tatou*," you hear that very often, "us, us, all of us." You are here to lift one another up. The Maori has pride in his skills and the ability to achieve, especially where work is concerned. The learning process is explicit. Where otherwise would you get your recipe for God, for instance, or what about science? That is all work. Maori begin all their speeches with, "God the creator, He is always supreme, always first above all else." Now, why cannot educated Pakehas come to grips with that?

How do you see the Maori feature in today's modern market?

He features badly for two reasons. He has never been taught adequate skills for the market. The Pakeha system made absolutely sure that our people were not schooled enough. For school certificate exams, fifty percent of our people do not pass, or are made sure not to pass. When you see our kids fail like that, you don't need to ask yourself why our people don't occupy higher-paid positions. The Maori are made to look inferior.

In what way do you think that the Waipareira Trust Village functions in Maori society today?

The Waipareira Trust comprises many tribes. It is important that we combine our efforts in doing things for Maori. We have learned to do that. At least we, Maori, have each other in the *whanau* system. The Pakeha has his work, and when he loses that, what has he got? A Maori goes back to his *whanau* on the *marae* when he loses his job and gets involved in duties there. When a Maori loses his job, his day will be structured along *whanau* lines—he will still be busy with other things. Maori adapt themselves. Our people are very innovative, and we know the value of work. To work is to survive. There are few Maori who would not look for work or create work. If there is no work, we create it.

The Account of Tom

Tom is the manager of a skills training centre that prepares Maori youngsters for the workforce by providing them with skills necessary for the building industry.

What motivates you to work, and what do you perceive work to be? What is it that you want from life, and how do you fit these objectives in a Maori context?

I grew up with a set of values that were given me by my mother, but these changed when she converted to another religion. Her values changed and became more Pakeha than Maori. She grew up with Maori values, but she changed her religion, and as a consequence her whole lifestyle underwent a transformation. Moreover, she wanted us to change from the Maori *whanau* concept taught by our dad to her new persuasions. But the most influential person in my life was my dad. Before this new religion came into my life, Dad taught me in Maori. He was an elder, a *kaumaatua*, and he lived our values. We had our own *marae*, but in the interest of the *whanau*, the *hapu*, and the *iwi*, the *marae* was moved to a certain place where one of the main leaders of the tribe was born. So we took the *marae* there, and there it remains.

The Puriwini is our *marae*—that is one of the main *maraes* up north. We are one of the biggest *iwi* of the New Zealand northern tribes. I am actually Nga Puhi, but my *hapu* is Nga Tehere.

My father taught me the basic values of life of the tribe, about what was right and what was wrong. And when I grew up, he taught me the facts of life. He told me about the changes that would take place in my body and that if I would get involved with a girl and she would fall pregnant, that he would make me marry her. Those values always stuck with me. Dad taught me no matter what it is that you do in your life, you stand up for it and accept the outcome.

How do the values of work in a Maori setting lead to all other aspects of Maori society?

When I grew up as a child, we were taught to work in the gardens. We had very big gardens, which took all the *whanau* that lived in the district to work in them. We had to plant the *kumaras*, we had to start right from the beginning, from the tubers. In other words, starting to grow the plants, you took the *kumaras* out of the pits and started with the planting. October was the time to plant, during springtime. During the winter you prepared the beds in which the plants had to grow, and planting started in spring. The thing you learned about it was the importance of food. You need food to survive.

When Dad grew up, there were eight in his family. His grandmother was the niece of the big chief Kaoti up in Northland, who was a big chief in Nga Puhi. She owned all the land in the valley. Dad was the youngest, the *potiki*, the one who carries on. Although the eldest was always looked up to, the youngest was the important person because he lives longer. The youngest is the worker. He also inherits the land because he continues longer than the eldest.

Who would then be more important, the children of the youngest or eldest sibling?

In the case of my dad, he was the youngest and he became the top elder in the tribe, but he only took that position when his eldest brother died. Now, the eldest son of the youngest brother, then, will be the elder. If he has no other brother and he dies, he loses the land to someone else in the tribe. It is a plan that is not written down anywhere—it is automatically done, you are not called to a meeting. Maori go to a *tangi* [funeral] or *mate* when someone dies. That is the only time that you see all your relations. When that time arrives, it is then that they will address you with your right title, because everybody understands the system.

When my grandfather came from England with the army, he met my grandmother, and in order for him to stay in New Zealand, he had to have a *waewae*, a place to stand on, some land for him to live on. What my grandmother did was to parcel off her land between her children and to keep enough for herself and her husband. My dad, who was the youngest, could have had all those three thousand acres. That was the way in which my grandfather obtained Maori status, because he now had *turangawaewae*, a place to stand on. Because grandmother was strong through connection with the chief, she needed to give her partner the same strength and, thus, she elevated him in status.

When we grew up I never knew my grandparents because they died before I was born. My dad became the *kaumaatua*, and whatever went on in the *hapu*, he dealt with it all. He was about thirty-five years old at the time. He had to deal with land and family issues and all other things. Thus, when I grew up I realized that this was the way that things were done, and that was the way that I did them. Our elders tell us, "We do not need your money. Things need to be done as they have been done for generations." It did not matter who you were, *ariki* [chief] or villager, you performed all the duties that were required of anybody. The people who left for the cities always come home for important ceremonies. They never lost that part of their learning. I can become a chief because my name belongs to the chiefs from way back, but you must earn the right to be *ariki*.

Where do differences manifest themselves in the work-force?

My people lived in the valley, what we knew as the valley. They went to the town to get jobs, but they had no skills, not the skills that were required for well-paying jobs. That is why they became good at road works, the freezing works, or the power board, because they did not need skills to do those jobs. You were told, "Pick up a post, stick it into the ground, and there you are." However, Pakeha did not understand that when someone died in the family, Maori went back home for a week. Pakeha organization did not mean a thing to them. What Pakeha work did mean was that you were needed at work, and that if you were a good worker, your employer might hold the job for you. If you were not, you missed out on the job. If that happened, you lapsed into poverty.

Poverty was the biggest common denominator when I was young. Because they had no money, they would fall back onto the safety net in the valley, they could come back to work in the big gardens. However, poverty in the city leads to all sorts of crime.

I went to school, but I still had not made up my mind as to what I wanted to do. We lived in the country, and five miles down the road was one of the biggest freezing works in New Zealand. In the summer they employed two thousand workers and about fifteen hundred workers all year round. Thus, dads and some of the sons would work at the freezing company, whereas the rest of the sons would be working on the farm, as my brother did. I also stayed home on the farm, but I did not like that work. There was always plenty to do back home, working the gardens, work on the *marae*. It was harder for a woman to be unemployed. For a man it was easier because there were set tasks to do, building a *whare* [house], fixing fences on the farm, and the like. For the man it was easier to come back with no job—you would be looked after, *awhi*, you were looked after. But at the same time they wanted you to look for a job, because what came to the table came from hard work in the community outside. You were encouraged to go back to the city to look for work.

What do you think is the reason that so many Maori fail in the Pakeha system?

It has nothing to do with laziness. Rather, the reason is that when we decided to leave the village for the big city, we were not warned about life in the urban centres. All you had heard from others was that in the city you could have all the fun you desired and that getting a job was very easy. Thus, all we thought about was to get a job and to get out of city living what we could in having a good time. We were not told about the skills to be required in order to get a job in Auckland. All you heard was, "I have a job for you on the power board," or "You can work on the roads for the city council." You had no problem getting one of those. You did not aspire to get more than what you needed and what you were comfortable with.

What ideas may urban Maori have developed about poverty in relation to urban standards?

I believe that poverty came to the country areas as a result of the government policies during the 1980s. The downfall occurred when the big freezing companies closed down one after the other, and that was the beginning of the end for Maori. The next thing was the construction industry that fell under the government's axe: "The quickest way to economize is that when a business is not economically viable, it should be reduced in size." The message to us was, "Stop, get off to the unemployment office for the dole." In Auckland, the big freezing companies were all but wiped out. Maori became unemployed, and once they were without a job, they realized what being poor really meant. Back in my day there was no unemployment. When you came to the city you got a job right away, working on the roads and the motorways. Maori were sought after in the construction industry. There are heaps of jobs in Auckland today, but what the government has failed to do is to give Maori the qualifications in appreciation of what they can do. This is one of the most difficult things for a Maori to understand, because they do not realize that they need a piece of paper to get a job.

Do you see the value of education systems, and did you have the same respect for your teachers as you awarded your kaumaatua?

No, because the schoolteacher was foreign. He looked foreign, he spoke foreign, and when you did not do what you were told, you were caned. I spoke Maori when I was young, prior to going to school. The difficult part was that you started to believe that you needed to speak English because you were told to do so and caned if you did not. My mother told me that if I did not do as I was told, God would consider me a sinner. If I went to the pub, I would commit sin. This concept was foreign to me—I could not relate to that. God made trees, the earth, the fishes, everything. The Pakeha God is one God—you cannot have ten gods. But Maori have more than one God. There is the God of the earth, the God of the forest, the sea, and so on. I relate to that. The other day I looked at a tree. Trees can grow with one another, even in the same spot. My comment is that those trees are living things. Some people may have different ideas, but they do not realize that they are living things. I learned about the environment when I was young. I learned that when you polluted the sea, it would not yield the food. If you polluted the rivers, you could not drink the water. For me it is difficult to learn that in the name of progress you pollute a whole river. This river provides entire families with the means of survival. But people just kill the whole river.

As I grew up, I never forgot my dad's values, but forgot those of my mother's new religion. When I moved to Whangarei, I made up my mind that I would never have anything to do with her faith again. I went back to Dad and my Maori roots. Through that religion, I saw the Pakeha way of life and the things that I did not agree with. Dad's values were based on those of the Ratana Church [Maori Christian Church] and the Church of England, but he also had the roots of his people in him, such as the gods of the sea and the forest and so on. He believed in a supreme being without whom nothing would happen. He related always to the truth, and would always say grace, give a blessing, always in Maori. When we planted things, he would pray. Mum would not do that and condemned such behaviour as paganism.

I would like to relate an incident. In the back of the farm we had *kauri* trees growing, something that a Pakeha wanted. I discovered that my dad was negotiating with this Pakeha who wanted to buy some of those trees. When I asked my dad what that money would be spent on, he replied that it would be allocated to building a *marae* for the *whanau*. That would be the actual payment, building that *marae*. No money passed hands. In reality, the Pakeha received three times the value in timber, as the value of the *marae* was minimal compared to the value of the rest of the *kauri* trees. The old people did not have any idea of the economic value of the trees—they were not schooled enough in those things. What they did know was that in order for the *whanau* to survive, the construction of the *marae* was essential. They made sure that whatever we needed at the marae was obtained, although they lost out considerably on the deal.

What I realize most today is that because there are two people in me, Pakeha know-how combined with Maori identity, I am now more on my guard when I enter into business negotiations. I realize that when I do business with a Pakeha, he is by himself. He may have all the skills behind him, but he is still by himself. Once upon a time, he could exclude Maori, but now he cannot, not in whatever he does. Because if he builds a building, he has to consider the Resource Consent [legislation to protect Maori property rights] in order to make sure that there rests no *tapu* on it, or that there may be trees on the property that he cannot cut down. He has to be careful today in his considerations. All those things they used to take for granted are no longer to be taken for granted. So they have to include me for either eliminating or working with me, as per legislation. In the past, a Pakeha may have said, "I want to build a house on that land over there and cut those trees." But not so today. He may find that there is a *waahi tapu* [burial place] on that land and he cannot go any further. In the past, he would have ignored it and built on it anyway. But now it is different—you can no longer continue to build on such land. A new cycle has started. It is the same in the city.

Can you tell me a little bit more about this development?

When I was born, I had a relationship with the land. So, all that we have has been passed down from generation to generation, such as living with the land as *tangatawhenua*, whereas the Pakeha would not relate to the land like that. Land to them has always been regarded as a commercial commodity, something related to profit. I am always related to the land. Whatever you take from the land, you give thanks to God. Now Pakeha are really starting to learn! When we talk about *wairua* [spirituality], we have been familiar with this concept for generations. Pakeha are just talking about it now. These are things that are important to human beings: the trees, the sky, the water. Pakeha are only now realizing that those things are important and that you cannot just take what you want from nature. *Tikanga* is the concept of birth, death, and living. It is the whole concept, and it ties in with the concept of work.

The New Zealand history of my lifetime, or of my generation, has been discarded by the Pakeha. The children of today receive all that they want to learn about Maori and what was taken away from us in the past and during my time. When I go back to my primary school days, I learned things about Maori, but when I got to secondary school, I learned nothing about it. I learned all about England and its history, but nothing about Maori. The young people of today are learning about New Zealand, but the education system is still trying to hide things by only revealing part of it. Changes have occurred in New Zealand society because of immigration from Asia and other countries over the last decades. Pakeha are now referring to New Zealand as a multicultural nation, but Maori has tried to tell them that ever since the Treaty of Waitangi was signed, we were a bicultural country with two peoples, Pakeha and Maori. Before you can sort out the multicultural thing, deal first with the bicultural aspect! The next fifty years will be most critical for Maori. Because of intermarriage, there are people with both our bloods running through their veins, and they are not going to ignore the other half of them.

I will also say something about the meetinghouse on the *marae*, because it is very important for Maori and it represents the way we think about ourselves as a people. The meetinghouse is constructed like a human body. The spine up top, everything radiates from there. Two poles in the middle represent the upper part and the lower part of the body. It represents a person crouching, or kneeling, on the ground— that is the position of the structure. It also gives recognition, more than recognition, to women. Without women, men cannot be here. All the way down the line, I have been taught, "Woman is most important, the main part." Man represents food. That is what I was taught when I was young. Men and women need each other in society. They contribute to the survival of the people, each in their own sphere.

A Maori Woman of the Maori Women's League

Rangi is a member of the Maori Women's League. She works for the NZQA and audits Maori private training establishments, including Tom's facility, for their effectiveness in preparing Maori youth for the workforce.

Your position in the public service includes the observation and supervision of Maori establishments. Do you find that the students' sense of being Maori is preserved as they prepare for the workforce and are exposed to the workings of the labour market rather than their own environments?

It depends on the *kaupapa* [policy] of that organization— they are as Maori as they want to be. NZQA will know by the end of the year how successful the program is for Maori.

Was your background entirely Maori? Has your way of thinking been shaped by other cultural aspects?

My mother was English and my father Maori. My parents were in the air force in London during WWII. They married and went back to New Zealand after the war and settled down in Wellington. In the chaos of post-WWII conditions, people were not informed on credit ratings, how to pay bills, and the like. This information had not been passed on to the next generation, which made life in the city very difficult. Thus, my parents decided to move up north, to Whangarei and whereabouts, which turned out to be very difficult and unsettling for my mother. Being a product of a mixed marriage, it meant for me that one culture needed to be surrendered or neglected. It was my *taha Maori* side that was not being valued, because being Maori at the time was not fashionable. My father changed his name from Matiu to Matthew because people had difficulty pronouncing it.

Was your mother's side stronger than your father's side, or did she have to adjust to the Maori way of doing things?

My mother had to adjust, but my father spoke the English language like an Englishman—that was a requirement for the air force. As a result, we never lived the formal side of being Maori. The old people were also telling us to learn to speak the English language: "Don't speak Maori, because you get beaten at school. You need to speak the Pakeha way." My father grew up at a time when they received beatings at school for speaking Maori. I have seen how that experience has affected the half-castes, and how the half-caste culture developed.

For my mother it was very difficult to have to share her home with everybody in a small town. As someone from the UK, she was used to having her own house, her own place to herself and her family. She found it difficult that people just dropped in and stayed for weeks. My mother's sister came out to New Zealand from England, and my siblings and I and our friends would never just drop in on her unannounced, which meant that the Maori side of the *whanau* never went to visit her. The case of *tapu* posed a problem too in the English environment, as the members of that household would wash their hair and clothes in the kitchen sink, where the dishes would also be washed, or dishes with food would be left. This is an affront to Maori cultural norms. Going out to dinner meant that the whole *whanau* would join in and prepare or bring food, whereas to the English side it meant to be eating finger foods and snacks. When an emergency occurred in my English aunt's home, the ambulance people came in, placed the sick person on a stretcher on the floor, and continuously stepped across the patient to strap him in. For Maori it is *tapu* to step across one's body—it has to do with the *mana* of that person. Even if it is a woman, you do not step across her body.

Could you tell me something about the function of the Maori Women's Welfare League?

The Maori Women's Welfare League is a big organization of Maori women who organize activities for welfare programs for Maori. They cater for prisoners and young people. They visit women in their homes and provide education programs for Maori. It is in this respect that the women feel that they are making more progress than the men. The Welfare League is a nationwide organization, and it has taken the lead in representing Maori women in Pakeha society and the care of those who need help, especially in matters of unemployment, health, and education. It also means that Maori women have lowered tribal boundaries to be able to work together and achieve their goals, something that would never have been considered before the mass migration to the cities. The Welfare League's involvement in Maori education has given rise to the Kohanga Reo movement, which caters for the education of Maori children in preschool programs and primary education.

* * *

Although all the participants of the last three chapters speak from varying perspectives, their accounts show how Maori institutions were severely damaged by Pakeha interference. Furthermore, all were adamant that regardless of Pakeha opinion on the matter, Maori grow up with an inherent work ethic fostered and nurtured from early childhood in the village and the *whanau* by the elders of their communities.

All participants mentioned that work and play in the Maori setting coincide with life learning. Children do not play in the sense that their Pakeha counterparts are encouraged to do, with time set aside specifically for entertainment. Since all villagers worked together, children as well as adults, work became play when children performed their duties together. Early childhood teaching about fishing, reading the winds and the ocean, and knowing when to plant and where, together with pride in ancestors, form the foundation of Maori beliefs and values and give rise to a work ethic that is culturally specific to Maori people.

The participants demonstrate that the spiritual essence of Maori thought and action features prominently in Maori ideational systems and their social institutions and relations. Their spirituality is manifest in the fact that all Maori activities are preceded with a *karakia*, or an incantation of a specific kind. The two *kaumaatua* insisted that the Pakeha label of "laziness" is not relevant to Maori people. On the contrary, the stigmatic term is misapplied when one considers that Maori children are taught the value of work at a very young age, whereas Pakeha children play and fully rely on their parents to provide them with all their needs.

Despite Tom and Rangi's work experiences in the public service, their work values arose from their upbringing in a predominantly Maori environment, although Rangi had been exposed to conflicting cultural practices at a very early age because of the English influence of her mother and her relatives. Tom's conflict stemmed from his mother's conversion to a Christian denomination with beliefs and values in direct opposition to the teachings of his father and his identity as a Maori. Tom reiterated other participants' descriptions about work for Maori in the freezing and other public works; during the 1990s, one freezing company after another closed its doors in the country towns and eventually in the urban centres, which created an economic and social disaster for many Maori workers.

The transformations in the labour market generated an ideology that advanced individualization and individual employment contracts and the requisite certification of skills. The move towards the individualization of the workforce proved to be disadvantageous for Maori workers, who were denied the opportunity of working side by side with other Maori. Men faced additional challenges, such as the possibility of working with women or experiencing a woman exercising authority over them.

Tom's reference to the way that farm and landholdings pass on to the youngest sibling in the family suggests there are decisive differences in Pakeha and Maori ideational systems in a range of aspects, despite the many programs that seek to accommodate Maori workers and give them equal opportunity to succeed in the Pakeha labour market. Both David and Tom have shown that progress for Maori people can only take place by Maori moving forward in their own way in those parts of the economic sector that are purposeful, valuable, and desirable to them.

Chapter 8
Other Cultural Considerations

In order to substantiate my findings regarding the claim that work means different things to different people, I have consulted Indian and Chinese sources on the Internet in order to gain a broader perspective on how people of different cultural backgrounds regard their entry into a globalised labour market and how it may affect their value and belief systems.

Previous chapters show that the principles of the Western work ethic contrast significantly with the values and beliefs about work of non-Western cultures, such as the Maori people of New Zealand, who provide a typical example of how indigenous people incorporate their economic activities in the overall structure of mainstream society while still keeping religious and other aspects of their social lives intact. The Maori elders I interviewed explained the Maori system as holistic, with all aspects of social life merging into a mutually conclusive whole, as opposed to Western thought, which is singular and tends to compartmentalise social institutions into different boxes.

Dr. Joseph J. Pallath asserts that the history of the whole world is a history of conflict between invading and original cultures. Almost as a rule, techniques employed by dominant cultures tend to marginalise those known by the original inhabitants, virtually destroying the way of life of indigenous people and replacing it with modern technology. The introduction of the market economy and the globalisation of the world of work have threatened rather than freed native cultures, whose values are undermined by the norms of consumer culture and whose cultural identities are destroyed in the process.

In India this process proved detrimental for the Dalits, tribal and fisher folk who were once known as Untouchables. The history of India contains a conflict between two cultures: the culture of the invading people (Savarnas) and the original inhabitants of the land (Avarnas). Historians and social scientists insist that the Dalits were at one time a tribal people conquered by the immigrants (Savarnas), whose lives and customs were absorbed by the invaders.

Pallath further explains that as globalisation proceeded, India's mainstream culture was swallowed up by consumer culture, which denies bio-cultural and technological diversity by imposing mono-technology upon society. Mainstream Indian culture, which ruthlessly imposed its rules on the simple lifestyles of the tribal and fishery people, is in turn being swallowed up by modern consumer culture. Thus, values such as cooperation, sharing, and generosity, which were generated by local technologies to satisfy basic needs for food and housing, are being so altered by modern technology that social and cultural systems are being destroyed.

We may ask at this stage if these changes in India's social and cultural world have also resulted in changes in Indians' work habits and behaviour in their workplaces and the wider community. Can we expect that business in India is being conducted along the same lines as in Western countries, and that consumer culture has altered ideational systems in such a way that workers in that country aspire to the same outcomes for their efforts in the workplace as their Western counterparts do? In a globalised market, do workers from different countries agree on every aspect of doing business because a liberalising market economy negates such factors as culture and religion?

The author suggests that negotiations between Western and Indian businesses tend to start well, until the representatives of the Western company make it clear that they expect the deal to be completed in one day, unlike their Indian counterparts, who refuse to be rushed into a decision, as they need to go back to their senior colleagues for approval. Such differences in approach often result in a degree of discomfort and mistrust between parties, who tend to consider each other with a measure of suspicion stemming from the different values and beliefs that they carry to the negotiating table. Trust, then, becomes a central issue between business associates who operate from different cultural aspects in their approach and expect a deal to be considered from their respective viewpoints.

Indians view time differently than their Western colleagues, which can lead to hours of debate on business deals without concrete decisions being reached. In the United States, adhering to deadlines is considered normal and expected. Contrary to Western ideas, Indians will give priority to family matters over work. Also, aggressive behaviour on the Western side of the negotiation table may be viewed as a sign of disrespect by the Indian side, which can lead to a complete lack of communication and motivation on their part. In order to foster and develop professional trust between the parties, representatives of Western businesses must take the time to get to know their Indian counterparts in order to have good business relations.

Pallath further insists that a cultural approach to the study of work patterns is rarely considered. Culture, or the ideational system of a people, is their way of life, their way of viewing the world they live in and their way of specifying their economic activities and the use of their environment, which gives rise to distinctive patterns of thought and behaviour. Culture is the way of life of a people and common to a society; it is the condition of being human. An in-depth study of the work patterns and behaviours of the Indian people would yield significant variations, therefore, in values and specific worldviews, those ideational patterns that guide them to choices and outcomes in their economic activities and characterise them as a society.

John, an American businessman, had been excited at the prospect of entering into a joint venture with a particular firm in Mumbai and was hopeful that the outcome would be of mutual benefit and prosperity. He expected that he would close the deal in a couple days and could quickly return to the US and start implementing the plans. However, his Indian counterparts noted his hurry to finalise the deal and became rather concerned with what they perceived as his impatience. They began to question his intelligence, abilities, and sincerity when he insisted on moving the procedures on as soon as possible without allowing them to consult their senior colleagues for advice and final approval.

If both parties had approached the conference table with the willingness to understand differences in doing business, it would have been clear that the ensuing problems did not stem from personal ambitions or character, but that they were based on variations in the cultural backgrounds of both parties, which resulted in misgivings about intentions on both sides.

As discussed earlier, in Western countries efficiency and adhering to deadlines are considered desirable qualities in the world of business. In India, such business traits are regarded as tokens of disrespect. As part of the process of doing business in India, one is bound to be invited to the prospective business partner's home, which requires taking a box of candy or a bunch of flowers in appreciation for the invitation.

I mentioned earlier the conflict of interests between Pakeha workers and the *mana* of Maori men, which is jeopardized when the latter need to work in close proximity with the former. Pallath points out that the modern Western pattern of development is based on a Western patriarchal value system, whereas the original culture of the state of Kerala in India, for instance, is predominantly matriarchal, which has distinct consequences for its social institutions.

In the Indian context, the simple cultures are the Dalits, the tribal and fisher folk. Although they represent more than 50 percent of the population, they still live a marginalised existence. After independence in 1947, the government took away a considerable amount of forest land, which had sustained tribal standards of living and provided basic needs. This action annihilated tribal cultures and ways of life. Moreover, the culture of the fisher people was largely destroyed as marine production was taken over by the local rich and multinationals. These events spelled the end of Dalit cultures, which were destroyed as their ways of life were replaced by modern technology and dominated by foreign ways.

The modern Western pattern of development in the world of work is a carrier of a patriarchal Western value system, and the matriarchal Dalit system, with its imaginative cosmic–mythic belief system, was no match for a more masculine and aggressive development pattern that had little place for religious values and passive feminine attitudes.

Contributions from an online survey on Indian work values yielded some interesting data. One participant suggested that Indian thinking is circular, in contrast to Western linear thought. He mentioned the concept of karma: what goes around comes around. Indian values and beliefs are embedded in this philosophy. This could also be compared to the *whanau* system of the Maori, in which economic and social thinking embrace the family and are never singular in essence.

Another discussant explained that when people migrate from India's rural areas to the cities, their cultural habits and behavioural patterns undergo drastic change. In rural areas, people live in close communities with close family bonds. Individual behaviour carries consequences for the collectivity, and family honour ranks in priority. On the other hand, city life tends to isolate the individual from close family ties, and individual goals and materialism replace principles of sharing. Nevertheless, the principle of karma is still deeply seated in most Indian minds, and promotes the ideas that people have been sent into the world to make a name for themselves and their families and that education is the key to success. Spiritual ideas lead to an overall acceptance of good and bad days, because that is the way that God works; life moves in cycles, and good follows bad.

Family remains important to Indians. The father is supposed to work hard to provide for the family, and the mother provides all the domestic support in order for the family to function well. The family is the prime reason for, and the centre of, all activities in and around the home, which is grounded in a strong spiritual foundation to foster the strength to overcome the eventualities that can beset a family.

Cultural differences often surface during business negotiations between Indians and Westerners, which often start well but result in misunderstanding as a result of cultural differences. Pallath asserts that trust in business situations is a central issue between parties, as both sides tend to develop serious doubts about the sincerity, capability, and trustworthiness of their counterparts. Thus, we see that cultural differences play a salient part in global market negotiations between people from the East and West.

Chinese Economic and Social Values

In my inquiry into Chinese work and value practices, I have leaned heavily on Guy Faure's essay "China: New Values in a Changing Society," which I obtained from the Internet. Not having had any experience in this society, I have relied on Faure's findings.

A globalised labour market must recognise that all its participants come from different social backgrounds, and that variations in dealing with economic issues influence business deals and work practices. This chapter examines Chinese work values as Western societies have absorbed vast numbers of Chinese workers and China has become a major player in the world economy. This inquiry is not designed to discuss the industrial development of that nation, but to examine the value and belief systems that give rise to cultural differences when doing business with the West. It is important, therefore, to look into Chinese history in order to arrive at some understanding of their practices and expectations in the world of work.

Guy Faure proposes that China's five-thousand-year-long history has undergone massive changes over the last twenty-five years, causing an incredible evolution of the values and beliefs of the people, especially of those in urban settings. However, to assume that there has been a swing or inversion of values, or a dramatic change in the nature of society, or that China is catching up with modern technology and Western trends, would be misleading, as new elements of the Western world are simply digested and finally reused within China's existing social system. In order to understand Chinese work and social practices, careful consideration of the cultural foundations of Chinese civilisation is essential. According to Faure, Chinese culture is commonly described as the complex product of three systems of thought: Confucianism, Taoism, and Buddhism.

Yu-Ping Wang clarifies that Confucianism traditionally encouraged the pursuit of long-term benefits as a trade-off for thriftiness. This philosophy stresses the value of diligence and hard work to achieve long-term goals, which can be related to the work values of self-enhancement and openness to change. The way of life in modern China is not much different from anywhere else in the world because of Western influence. However, tradition still lingers in all Chinese households and communities worldwide. In rural areas in China, the traditional way of life is very much alive still. Although the conditions of life have changed, long-established values of family importance and reputation are still upheld by all Chinese families.

Faure argues that China and the West have contrasting models of intellectual processes. He observes that Westerners have developed an analytical approach to problems, separating and dealing with them individually when required. The Chinese, on the other hand, have developed a global perception, or holistic approach to dealing with problems.

Western reasoning tends to be linear, following either an inductive process from facts to conclusion, or a deductive approach by considering information or evidence carefully in order to find the solution to a problem. In contrast, the Eastern way of reasoning can be more accurately described as an inverted system of concentric circles, which slowly move from the edge to the core of the subject.

In negotiations, the Chinese use concrete reasoning, metaphors, proverbs, stories, and traditional adages to explain the whole of the picture, along with its ambiguities and contradictions. Western thinking aims to be objective, separating facts and judgement, whereas Chinese thinking expresses the need to evaluate, judge, and take a side in any situation. In other words, in Chinese thought, there is good or bad; behaviour is either correct or wrong, there is no neutral position. The behaviour of any foreigner working with Chinese is thus constantly being evaluated. If there is balance in thinking, contradictions can be reversed, opening up a wide range of possible actions for all parties involved.

According to Faure, Chinese society is characterised by prominent basic values of face saving, indirect action, and centrality. Chinese people appear to be preoccupied with reputation, especially concerning one's own behaviour and that of the family. To lose face or feel humiliated is the worst thing that can happen to one's person. Maintaining face takes priority over providing a correct answer. As Faure states, "The regulating mechanism of social behaviour is the feeling of shame instilled in the mind of every Chinese. Face may not only be enhanced but also traded by giving face to the counterpart, who in turn has to reciprocate." In relationships, things are suggested, not told straightforwardly. Thus, replying with a direct "no" in a discussion would be perceived as a clear lack of good manners.

Faure further states that in the tough, merciless global Chinese society, there is no room for trust; suspicion is, rather, the norm. Trust in business has to be built, starting with the establishment of a relationship between friends and relatives with whom business can be carried out at low risk. This explains the eagerness of the Chinese to develop personal networks or to rely on the family. As for the concept of centrality, the Chinese mind operates from concentric circles, with China positioned as the centre of the world. Such centrality applies to cultural views, with the point of reference being Chinese views, values, and foods, which suggests that a strong sense of cultural superiority is ingrained in the Chinese mind. The Chinese character for "China" literally translates as "The Middle Kingdom," because the Chinese have always held their culture in high esteem, viewing it and their nation as lying in the centre of human civilisation.

Over the last decades, changes have taken place in China, not only in the economic and technical domains, but also in other levels of Chinese society. A great percentage of the population of China is exposed to Westerners through joint ventures or foreign-owned enterprises, which has stimulated increased interaction among people. The learning process that has taken place has caused considerable change in Chinese society, not only in the economic situation but also in the depth of Chinese personality and values. Younger generations of Chinese workers have become individualistic and materialistic, seeking more challenges and change in the pursuit of better employment opportunities and higher wages. Family values are challenged in many aspects when a son or daughter who has studied abroad earns a salary twenty times higher than that of the father. This may indicate that personal interest and individual need are becoming more prioritised, and that reference groups such as the family may no longer feature prominently in personal decision making.

Would it, therefore, be reasonable to assume that since attitudes toward economic and social issues are changing in China, Chinese work relations and industrial arenas will develop along Western ideas in the future? It appears that there are crucial differences between Western values and attitudes in the world market and those of China, which developed in virtual isolation over five thousand years. Again, it would be quite mistaken to expect that a changing Chinese society would develop mind-sets commensurate with Western-style values and expectations, and that, therefore, business negotiations between Chinese and Westerners will be conducted within the frame of Western ideals.

The Mormon Perspective

An investigation into work ethic would not be complete without considering a third possibility, one that could demonstrate elements of both sides of economic thought: a Western perspective with tribal elements. To this end, I have inquired into the industrial practices of a religious group that has spread around the globe over nearly two hundred years and has maintained its distinctive values, beliefs, and social institutions with only slight variations across culture groups. There is substantial evidence to support the argument that the Latter-day Saints, also known as Mormons, adhere to a distinct worldview that originated in the Salt Lake Basin and spread around the world without visible loss of basic concepts and forms of beliefs. This worldview is strengthened by a church government that is highly centralised and promotes unification as the ideal form of development for its members.

Although Mormons are now dispersed throughout the world and local cultural variations may differ from the Utah version, their most basic expressions are clearly found not in the physical or social realms, but in the conceptual, which involves an ideology that encompasses a specific worldview.

John Sorenson, an anthropologist, specifies that a worldview is characterised by a reasonably standardised explanation of the meaning of life and the universe, shared values, and a set of facts. After the Civil War in the US, the Mormons were regarded as a rebellious people and were required to surrender their separate political and cultural identity through integration into a capitalist economy and to pledge loyalty to American institutions. Yet in the twenty-first century, Mormons continue to see themselves as separate from their mainstream societies, due to a worldview which is unique to them and which sets them apart from other social and religious groups, as their social institutions are founded upon religious beliefs.

To gain some understanding of the organisation of the institutions of the Mormons, it is necessary to explain that beneath family life and social structure lies the basic concept of Eternal Progression, which asserts that life does not cease at the end of mortal existence. Mormons hold this view in common with Christians from other denominations, as discussed earlier in the teachings of John Calvin. However, the concept of Eternal Progression also includes a continuation of a preordained plan of eternal growth and education and the principle of eternal marriage, by which husband and wife are sealed together with their children and ancestors in an eternal family unit. This principle forms the platform for the Plan of Salvation, which is governed by the Melchizedek, the higher priesthood.

The cultural expression of the Mormon worldview was intensified in the Great Basin in western North American in the second half of the nineteenth century, when the Saints enjoyed fifty years of isolated, undisturbed existence. Today, Mormons throughout the world stay in close contact with their central leadership in Salt Lake City. The worldwide church is divided into local stakes and wards, each a microcosm of the main organisation, which receives its directions from church headquarters in Salt Lake City. Each unit's priesthood quorums are patterned on the Priesthood Authority of the First Presidency of the Church and the Quorum of the Twelve Apostles. To complement the works and efforts of the priesthood holders, the women of the church are organised in corresponding auxiliary units, with the General Relief Society Organisation in Salt Lake City under the direction of the First Presidency of the Church.

Prophets past and present in the Church of Jesus Christ of Latter-day Saints have counselled the members of the church that no system can help them into a position where they can help themselves, become self-reliant, and become thus a free and independent people. This great principle, however, does not deny the needy and the poor or the assistance they should have. Church doctrine promotes the principle that man is an agent to himself only if he is self-reliant and independent, which are critical keys to his spiritual growth. Whenever one gets into a situation that threatens one's self-reliance, one finds his freedom threatened also. Nevertheless, the doctrines of the church promote interdependence between those who have and those who have not because of unforeseen circumstances. Members of the church are urged by their leaders to continually invest in their personal development and expand their occupational horizons by continued study.

Work is an essential element in the church's welfare program, as its results solve the temporal needs of the worthy poor, and bless and sanctify the labour of the labourer. The recipient of the welfare program accepts assistance in the spirit of gratitude, knowing that the time will come when he or she will, in turn, be able to contribute services to others. In this way, dignity and self-respect are preserved. All Latter-day Saints have the responsibility to provide for themselves and their families; this principle also applies to the priesthood. This widely heralded welfare program was instituted during the Depression in the early 1930s with the purpose of giving every member an intensified interest in his brother's welfare. It places an obligation of mutual support upon both the weak and the strong. There must be abundant charity, but no almsgiving.

In earlier chapters, we saw that in Western societies the terms *work* and *employment* are deeply embedded in our everyday speech, as the Western work ethic advocates that work is good in itself and stresses work as one's duty to society. The Protestant work ethic sanctioned the limitless accumulation and reinvestment of capital through hard work and, therefore, gave profit making a moral justification. Over time, the religious aspects of the beliefs and attitudes of the work ethic were gradually replaced by the expectation that hard work coincided with the norms of Western culture, which promised economic rewards as a result. In the Latter-day Saints' model, work is also morally justified as a duty to society and God; however, in this context, work ethic is inspired by religious beliefs and values that advocate that those who have should consecrate their plenty and give to those in need. Mormons are required to tithe 10 percent of their income to the church to further its programs, and to undertake a daylong fast once a month to contribute the money saved on meals to the church's fund to assist the poor. Those who obtain essential items from the church's welfare system are expected to put in some hours of effort to reciprocate for services and goods received. The church's welfare system in Utah boasts its own factories and canneries in which members who are temporarily out of work or permanently disabled find employment to cater for their needs.

Although the Protestant work ethic and Mormon values and beliefs about work advocate that work is good in itself, the two systems vary considerably in the desired outcomes of economic effort. Both models encourage the personal accumulation of wealth, but to different ends. In the Mormon instance, hard work is encouraged as a means for all members to provide for their own families, but also to help meet the needs of those less fortunate and give them the opportunity to resume their places in the workforce. Accumulation is encouraged, but not without the responsibility to consider those who are sick or temporarily unable to help themselves. This system implies that work involves not only payment for effort, but also many hours of effort spent outside official working hours without pay.

Chapter 9
Anomalies in the World of Work

My research into the world of work shows the way in which culture can be categorized, and how, as a result, transformations in the global labour market over the last decades are slowing the desired outcomes of neoliberal policies. Limited outcomes are occurring because the ideational systems of many Pakeha and Maori people are slow to adapt to what are often intensely problematic outcomes of such policies. New work practices are slow to accommodate technical innovation, causing a rift between contemporary ideologies of the labour market and the ideas and expectations that people have about their work. Labour market reforms have affected the ideational systems that govern people's cultures, rendering their work ethic at odds with contemporary market ideologies that promote the interests of the individual rather than those of the wider community or group. Thus, the changes in the labour market have disrupted the lives of workers whose previously standardized and predictable work conditions were forcibly removed in favour of individualized work contracts and marketable skills. The transformation in labour market processes and conditions have threatened the public culture of all participants in the labour market, but particularly those workers who have been marginalised as a result of failure to effectively adjust to contemporary market conditions.

For instance, modern market policy has negatively affected Maori work practice because its ideology actively encourages individual ambition and self-promotion and counteracts the collective ideas and practices to which Maori have traditionally adhered, whereby the interests and needs of the group are considered paramount. This study is helpful for indentifying the inconsistency between people's collective standards and beliefs about work and contemporary market ideology, which promotes individual drive and ambition and the satisfaction of individual goals and expectations. In other words, the conditions of the world of work are paradoxical; the ideology of market processes contravenes majority-held ideas about work and fails to recognize the needs of indigenous people, non-Westerners, and subgroups of Western societies, whose beliefs and values about work require different criteria for meeting economic and social needs.

Contemporary labour market transformations have impinged on people's beliefs about their work, creating a fundamental conflict of interest between the powerful, who are in the position to impose policies, and the powerless, who are left in a vulnerable position in the workforce. Hence, people's expectations about work are in conflict with the reality of contemporary labour market processes, as there is no longer a link between labour market ideology and working people's ideational systems. This conflict of interests is clear from my interviews with mainstream New Zealanders and Maori participants, who articulated how their values and beliefs have been undermined by neoliberal market policies.

By arguing that human work is socially defined and shaped, I exemplified how the work context of a society shapes the experiences of workers, and how the socially and culturally shaped ideational systems of members of a community coterminously shape the work context. I also showed how the data collected from participants are consistent with the views expressed, and how these views have been articulated through experiences that are anchored in and shaped by cultural perceptions.

Anthropological theory was useful for interpreting the reactions of my participants to the transforming forces of a globalising market. The work ethic and Fordist conditions in Western nations prior to the information age were social norms for workers and employers and were collectively observed by the majority of people in the labour market.

My research attempts to understand the implications of economic activity, how it is integrated into broader social systems, and how it is inscribed by the values and beliefs of members of different communities in New Zealand, and consequently the wider Western world.

The destructive effects of transforming market forces upon participants in the labour market were articulated by all my participants, who described their sentiments, emotions, and personal experiences and suffering. My Maori participants, although they were subject to the same labour market forces as their Pakeha counterparts, expressed the culturally specific solutions they found to the disadvantages they experienced in the job market.

I recognise the fact that we can only experience our own life and not that of another, even though we may receive clues about other people's actions and interpret them from our own perspective. My example of market transformation in New Zealand shows that mainstream New Zealanders and Maori people perceive the world of work through their own ideational systems and experiences in the labour market. It also demonstrates how cultural differences have shaped expectations, life ambitions, and goals for the two groups.

Contemporary interpretive theory has also been a tool in overcoming some of the difficulties in understanding other peoples' life experiences, how actors in the workforce have reacted to labour market reforms, and how these have corroded people's collectively held beliefs and values about work. Humans not only engage in activities, but also shape their actions according to their lived experiences, which differ from those of others who do not share the same circumstances due to the specific cultural context in which they occur.

The differences between the Japanese and British firms showed how identical technological and industrial environments created different labour organizations and industrial relation systems as a result of distinct variations in experience in the world of work and the collective beliefs of their workers. This example supported my discussion of the differences between the experiences of Pakeha and Maori people in the same workplace and provided me with a sounding board for my field data. All my participants were affected by the same market conditions, but the consequences for each group of people were dichotomised between individual experiences and collective perceptions that, in turn, gave rise to a search for solutions and outcomes guided by incompatible ideational systems. They are incompatible because people's expressions of experiences contain social units of meaning. While there is a problem in the relationship between experience and the way in which it is expressed, the interpretation of collected data provided a means to analyse my participants' expressed experiences by placing them in their cultural context.

Maori Beliefs that Shape Their Work Practices

My Maori participants had all spent their early childhood in the rural areas of New Zealand, where they spoke Maori as their first language and where they were instructed by their elders in the beliefs and practices of the *whanau* system, which mandates that the members of the group work and live for the good of the entire group. My participants insisted that ambition as a principle is, with noted exceptions, virtually unknown to Maori people, as the prime factor of their actions is anchored in the principle of *awhi mai te whanau*, pulling someone else up with you rather than progressing on your own. The rule implies the involvement of the elders of the *whanau* or *hapu* sitting in consultation with their charges and always referring to how things were done by their ancestors, whose decision making and actions continue to influence the members of contemporary Maori society.

The distinctions between individualistic Western thoughts about work contrast significantly with holistic Maori views of their work and society, especially in view of the *tapu, mana*, and *noa* considerations that shape the division of labour and all social considerations in all Maori activities. These distinctive factors comprise a critical divergence between individualized Western enterprise and collective Maori purposes for economic undertakings.

This divergence is manifest in irreconcilable attitudes toward ownership and possession of the land, which in a Western market can be bought and sold as any other commodity. Matiu and Aporo, the two *kaumaatua*, contended that Maori identity is closely connected with the land, which embodies genealogical links with ancestors and gods and binds the members of the tribes together as *tangata whenua*, who use their resources jointly. The distinct view of the worth and significance of the land continues to be a bone of contention between Pakeha and Maori, whose views remain diametrically opposed on social as well as economic grounds. Excessive land purchase during the early colonial years put Pakeha and Maori in direct opposition to each other in the contest for land and other valuable resources, as the former aimed to obtain as much as possible and the latter resisted all sales of land. The Maori attitude toward their land is as strong as the tie between a mother and her child; it is a bond that, according to my Maori participants, cannot be broken. Land, therefore, is to be handed down to succeeding generations and cannot be disposed of for personal gain. Adam expressed this feeling when he referred to his ancestor Te Kooti, who was involved in the resistance movements against land sales and whose deeds and achievements are still being recounted by his descendants.

The rise in landlessness was a key socioeconomic dynamic for Maori to migrate to the urban centres. Jan, Peta, and Mauri provided many insights into the changes in lifestyle and circumstances brought upon the Maori people. Jane pointed to the contrast of rural and city living regarding food: in the village, *tapu* is observed on food and produce from gardens, while in the city, all types of food is regularly available, which negates the *tapu* restriction in many aspects of everyday life. Life in urban areas requires that a Maori couple live with their children in one household, which causes relations in those families to become strained, as parents for the first time are forced together with each other and their children in a confined area rather than in separate areas on the *marae* in which *tapu* restrictions are observed. In such a case, *tapu* restrictions are severely compromised, as men are required to work together with their wives in the home, doing chores and taking care of the children because the *kaumaatua* had stayed behind in the villages.

Jane and Peta commented on the relative freedom that children were allowed on the *marae*, as opposed to the many restrictions that were imposed upon them in the city. Consecutive governments expected Maori people to fully integrate into mainstream society, but Maori people felt disenfranchised of all rights to pursue their own objectives, live their culture, and speak their own language. Mauri referred to her upbringing in the village in a household where her great-grandfather and his wife had occupied prominent positions as a result of his status as *tohunga* and her descent from such a line. They had taught her valuable principles, which she used to her advantage when she came to the city. Mauri's story accentuates the dilemma of the *mana* restriction for Maori in the urban situation by showing that she as a Maori woman, being *noa*, was less affected by the conditions in the Pakeha workforce. All participants agreed that Maori men are limited in their actions in Pakeha society because of the danger that their *mana* could be affected by working alongside women or taking orders from a woman.

My Maori participants referred to labour in the freezing works as a continuation of the *whanau* principle of living and working among relatives, being able to see them and touch them and creating real relationships in the workplace rather than the impersonal conditions in Pakeha work environments. Adam stressed the concept of *wairu* (spirit), which needs to flow from these relations in close proximity, and the idea of putting out one's hand to pull another person through in order to share success and prosperity.

In contrast, the principle of spirituality has mostly disappeared from the contemporary Western labour market. The religious basis of the work ethic has made way for hard work in an environment that stresses individual progress and ambition. Maori social and economic action, on the other hand, is still preceded by *karakia* (prayer) and other incantations in order to invoke the blessings of gods and ancestors on any undertaking.

My study draws attention to differences in the meaning of work as expressed by the actors in the world of work, whose values and beliefs about work vary according to their positions. Employers and managers of companies expect that workers be committed to company goals and requirements while also reserving the right to minimize operational costs by reducing staff numbers when necessary and often at will. In contrast, workers who still cling to the guarantees of the Fordist era feel frustrated by the changes that have occurred in the labour market, as their expectations of work are based on an ethic that has become obsolete and has been replaced by ambitions for personal gain. For them, the meaning of work has become arbitrary in an environment that steadily corrodes their bargaining rights and stability in the workplace and the quality of their working lives.

Individual employment contracts also denote an end to collective bargaining procedures. Mark, an employer, is well aware of the consequences of the contemporary rules in the labour market when he admits that many professionals will leave their places of employment for better conditions and prospects, which leaves employers no option but to actively compete with others for valuable skills. Many workers have experienced a loss of loyalty in the workplace as a result of the dismissal powers of employers, which only adds to their feelings of insecurity. The volatile conditions in the labour market have contributed to greater mobility of the workforce, as ambitions for advancement and profits are now pursued on both sides of the industrial spectrum. Thus, participants from both ends of the employment scale express the notion in the contemporary world of work, all parties in the workforce view each other with increased distrust, including the Maori people of New Zealand, who are seeking solutions that are meaningful for them.

That Maori people are seeking their own solutions was demonstrated by Adam, who explained the notion of "streetwise," a concept that defies the Pakeha rule of "doing the right thing" but which for Maori people carries the overriding principle of being able to take care of the members of the *whanau*. My Maori participants claimed that with the intervention of Pakeha in their way of life, the institutions that structured their society, their "perfect triangle," were upended by the demand that Maori were to do things the "Pakeha way," a way that is devoid of meaning for them. Hence, being "streetwise" enables Maori people to seek solutions for adverse labour market conditions in their own way. It protects Maori in many ways from *mana*-compromising situations as long as they do not get caught. If they are caught, rules of *mana* and *tapu* are threatened because, as Adam showed, joblessness and its stigma have different social meaning for Pakeha and Maori.

Transformations in the labour market followed by mass redundancies caused despair among workers, especially among those whose skills were declared obsolete. The meaning of work can be observed from the way people react to the consequences of new labour ideologies. For mainstream workers, the isolating individualism of neoliberal policies caused bewilderment and frustration at being treated as commodities and evaluated solely by the marketability of their skills. The downside of individuality means that one stands alone in a labour market in which competition for jobs is fierce and the rights of individuals are measured by how valuable their skills are for the company. In contrast to the collective nature of Maori society and customs, the individual in the labour market stands on his or her own, and their ability to fare well in the work arena depends on his or her bargaining power and skills.

For Maori, success is not measured by one's job and skills but one's standing in their community. Alienation in the Maori world results in what David terms the "failure to keep the paths back to the *marae* trimmed and to involve the *kaumaatua* in one's plans." The concept of time also means different things to Pakeha and Maori. For the former, it is valuable in terms of money and calculated by how it is used for future prospects and goals, while for the latter, it is measured in terms of past events by the acts and teachings of ancestors rather than ambitions for the future. Matiu and Aporo emphasized the term *tatou tatou*, which embraces the concept of inclusion of all members of the *whanau* and *hapu*, including ancestors, in every consideration, as well as the concept of work, which requires them to work together to benefit the entire group. Adam referred to the efforts by the government to keep urban Maori and the elders apart in an attempt to integrate urban Maori into Pakeha institutions and absorb them into mainstream society, which acts to individualise the Maori people and break up *kotahitanga*, the concept of Maori unity and separate development. David alluded to this process when he stated that Pakeha have attempted to decide what is best for Maori by creating programs intended to upgrade Maori ability to adjust to market conditions. He felt that as a result, Maori have become suspicious of such efforts and have continuously resisted them, despite their potential benefits.

Wealth acquisition, an important factor in labour market participation, has failed to become a significant issue for Maori as individuals, unless such endeavours are for the collective benefit of their people. David explained the Maori concept of poverty by noting that a poor Maori would be one with no contact with family or *whanau*. In contrast, poverty for Pakeha is measured by what he or she has or is deprived of as a result of the failure to procure a well-paying job or certain lifestyle.

David argued that the Treaty of Waitangi specifies the rights of two peoples to maintain their individual cultures and sovereignty, allowing them both to develop along their distinct cultural paths. He declared that, rather than dictating what is good for Maori, the government should ask what goals Maori groupings wish to achieve and then assist accordingly. David contended that although Maori are not ready to launch themselves globally, they are on the road to recovery, as they are strengthening their social institutions and taking a step forward as a people united in their objectives. A key difficulty lies in the sensitivities required when crossing tribal boundaries, but Maori have always aspired to self-development and self-government. David referred to mobilizing efforts made in educational fields, such as medicine, science, and information technology, in the move to serve their own people and to progress in the contemporary labour market with culturally specific and sensitive projects.

The meaning of work in the context of the two key peoples in New Zealand, the Maori and the Pakeha, is constructed within a common labour market. The market, in turn, constructs actors informed by distinct ideational systems who, as a result, have created beliefs and values about work that are distinct and representative of their respective ideational systems. The meaning of work for each social grouping has developed within divergent ideational systems that are anchored in different histories, originated in different environments, and evolved in different social, cultural, political, and economic circumstances.

While work ethics change as the needs of a society change, they do so over time. Sadly, the swift transformations wrought by the globalising labour market and internal socioeconomic policies in New Zealand have affected all working people, who have had to find solutions to the ensuing problematic social consequences of many ill-conceived policies in their own way and in their own time. Western workers, skilled and unskilled, have become highly mobile either by choice—being able to sell valuable skills in the market—or by force—frequently changing jobs due to dismissal and restructuring processes. Maori people also fell victim to contemporary labour market conditions when their collective work environments in the freezing and road works came to an end and the individualisation wrought by market forces and skill demands required them to fend for themselves in an unsympathetic job market. However, rather than re-skilling for future job preparation, Maori have opted to become "streetwise" by making use of their own networks to provide them occasionally with a few days of work while remaining dependent on WINZ for regular income.

It is clear that work is an important component of life and survival skills for both Maori and Pakeha, but each group expresses its ideational system and its consequent construction of the importance of work in varied and culturally specific ways.

Chapter 10
Building Bridges of Communication

I started this book with the definition of work ethic as a system of beliefs about work inherent to people of a specific culture or background; in other words, how people think about work, how these perceptions guide their subsequent behaviour in their places of work, and how they organise their work relations. This discussion led to two distinct streams of thought in the West:

1. Material historicism by Karl Marx, who saw the historical process as proceeding through a necessary series of modes of production characterised by class struggle and culminating in Communism.
2. The perspective of Max Weber, who insisted that Calvinism had developed a set of beliefs that morally justified profit making through hard work. This view led to the premise that being out of work was to be considered sinful. It gave rise to the Protestant work ethic and ultimately led to the replacement of mercantile capitalism by industrial capitalism, through which knowledge came to be applied to tools, processes, and products. This development ultimately caused work to shift from an aspect of the social sphere to the centre of society, and placed the responsibility for securing a position in the labour market squarely on the individual whose beliefs and values would require personal ambition and suitable skills.

The examples of different cultural viewpoints in the world of work have demonstrated the importance of considering traditional ways of organizing and structuring work and workplaces, as well as the traditional technology by which it was, and still may be, carried out. The Indian model showed how tribal people provided their basic needs of food and housing, and how these elements gave rise to their material as well as well as social and symbolic culture. The changes imposed on the tribal societies in order to accustom them to a modern consumer market and individual job opportunities in a globalising market destroyed their way of life and threatened their belief and value systems. Thus, any intervention into the conditions of a community should be preceded by extensive studies into the ways of living of the people in question. In the Mormon case, integration into mainstream society in the United States of America was inevitable, but even here cultural views and social organisation have persisted in Mormon societies worldwide.

Evidence has made it clear that when Westerners discuss the workings of a globalising labour market, they presuppose that workers from different cultural backgrounds have begun to think and act in terms and value concepts that are commensurate with Western standards and norms. This way of thought presupposes that business negotiations around the conference tables in all nations of the world should run according to Western-approved procedures. The reports in this book have demonstrated that non-Westerners approach the negotiating table with their own sets of beliefs and values about work and the rules and culture constructs of their respective societies.

In the first chapter, I introduced the concept of *meaning* as the key factor in a process that demonstrates how behaviour patterns and economic organisation are outcomes of the cultural constructs humans form as they make sense of their environments and organise themselves into actions that correlate with their perceptions. It is meaning that motivates choices within the framework of a society's institutions. As all humans need to provide for their existence and carry out all economic activities either for or with others, work is to be considered as essentially a social activity. However, as all need to work in various capacities and circumstances, it is false to assume that in a globalised labour market, industrial activity and work environments have taken shape along the same lines worldwide.

In Western societies, the developments in the world of work have altered the work ethic in such a way that its ideals are now at odds with its religious roots and accepted norms. In other words, the work ethic itself has become problematic for post-industrial society, as workers can no longer rely on work conditions based on norms and standards accepted by all factions of society. Work is regarded as the most important aspect of people's lives, and thus the right to work is regarded as of concomitant significance. The principle that "work is good in itself" became widely endorsed, stressing the need to work as one's duty to society. Work is perceived as a crucial part of the social contract for which the individual, in turn, receives certain rights and protection. It is this latter part of the social contract that is now at odds with most citizens of Western societies, who have come to feel disenfranchised in the world of work as their rights to work, and participation in society as contributing members, are steadily being eroded through unstable work environments, unexpected mass redundancies, and diminishing rights to work. Therefore, the notion of work as social contract in post-industrial times is rather ironic, as enforced idleness through loss of job seems to be the price that many pay for improved efficiency.

Anthropological research bases its premises on the fact that human beings make choices in their lives that are not exclusively concerned with economic activity but are consistent with the norms and standards of all other institutions of the societies they live in. Therefore, discussions about work in a given society need to consider cultural context in order to understand the way that people organise their places of work, how they think about their economic activity, and how their social institutions give rise to these thought and behaviour patterns. As discussed earlier, culture forms the framework for the beliefs and values by which humans define their world and their roles within it. It is the vehicle by which they give meaning to and guide their actions. Thus, work patterns and actions demonstrate a distinct view of the world unique to people of a specific society or nation. This implies that a discussion of globalisation must come to terms with issues of the variant rights, expectations, understandings, and entitlements that constitute the outcome of values and beliefs that have been forged in Western and non-Western backgrounds. Behaviour patterns in work environments show different outcomes as a result of differences in the expectation of rewards for social and economic effort.

The globalisation of markets in Western-oriented contexts has enabled women to occupy positions in the workforce that were previously only allocated to men, such as positions of leadership, and has led to men and women working together in offices and other workplaces. However, we have seen that for Maori men in the modern workplace, working in close proximity to women poses a serious problem, as traditionally Maori men and women were separated by rules of *tapu* and *noa* and a strict division of labour. Maori men are specifically disadvantaged in the labour market, as their *tapu* status restricts them from integration into mainstream work conditions and environments.

Dore's description of the Japanese example illustrates that despite nearly identical conditions in the manufacturing of virtually identical goods, the workers of British and Japanese firms had not organised themselves along comparable lines. On the contrary, their systems of operation showed distinct differences in development and concept, notably the lifetime commitment of the Japanese workplace versus the contractual relationship of the British workplace. In the Japanese system, a worker's family was considered a peripheral part of the company family, whereas in the British system, a man's role as employee was sharply divided from his roles as a husband, father, or individual outside the factory gates. One must accept, however, that Japanese labour and social conditions have changed over the last decades, as have those of the West. Over time, a sense of individualism has also raised its head in Japan, but to expect that those changes have been patterned on Western ideas would ignore an ancient cultural heritage and history. While Japan is regarded as a modern Western country, its industrial relations system has demonstrated that not all ideas about work serve the same purposes and goals, and the relations between workers and their places of work are not necessarily based on the same principles.

Equally, neoliberalism has enforced changes on Western labour markets by imposing norms and values on workers that impinge upon their traditional expectations of rewards for work. Expectations and previously guaranteed places in the workplaces of industrial society no longer correspond with the reality of conditions. I used the term *paradoxical* earlier to show the inconsistencies between workers' expectations and the real in the world of work, especially in light of mass redundancies and a volatile, often exclusive job market. However, the term *paradoxical* can also illustrate the differences between what Westerners expect of their work experiences and what non-Westerners regard as the norms and standards in their work and social environments.

Close inspection of these differences in expectations has shown that members of Western societies regard their participation in the world of work as an individual responsibility toward their families and societies and a matter of personal choice. On the other hand, for the Maori people of New Zealand, beliefs and thoughts about work are entrenched in all aspects of social life, merging them into one mutually conclusive whole. I showed that Maori identity, through a sequence of myth, tradition, and history, links people to ancestors and provides them with a holistic view of the world in which they live. The concept of *tapu* imposes strict rules of participation in society and a division of tasks that are still observed to such an extent that they considerably restrict the involvement of Maori men in the workforce.

These cultural restrictions have become a measure by which mainstream New Zealanders denigrate Maori workers as uncommitted to the work effort. Many Pakeha argue that Maori enjoy equal opportunity in mainstream society but are too lazy to take advantage of it. The question to be asked is, what exactly does the labour market in New Zealand offer the Maori, and what advantages are Maori people reluctant to take advantage of?

I wrote this book, therefore, with the sole aim of informing employers and workers that people of different cultures tend to view the concept of work through different-coloured glasses, and therefore no one work rule will apply to all workplaces in the same way. For this purpose, I used the ideational systems of Maori and Pakeha in New Zealand and their attitudes towards work as an example of how non-Western and indigenous people around the world react to a globalising labour market. To this same end, I supplied a history and explanation of the Western work ethic, tracing its development through decades of social, industrial, and technological change. Governments in Western countries such as New Zealand and Australia have assumed that all actors in the market, irrespective of cultural background, aspire to the same rewards for their industrial activities as a result of similar ambitions and life expectations. Consequently, market policy makers have enacted legislation concerning workers without considering different ideational systems in relation to work, different social relationships within the workplace, and contrary outcomes for indigenous people who do not constitute a significant part of the mainstream society created by the people who colonized their country.

Western societies include minority groups, including indigenous people, whose cultural backgrounds differ in values and beliefs about work and whose response to labour market forces may take a different course in order to meet their needs, as my example of the Maori people has shown. Hence, work means different things to different people, and actors in the labour market do not aspire to the same expectations, outcomes, and rewards for their economic efforts.

The changes that have taken place in the world of work, particularly those in New Zealand during the 1990s as a result of the development of information technology, have provided an example of the transformations in local and global labour markets. Prior to the information age, social obligations were embedded within labour contracts that divided the day between time at work and obligations to family and home. In other words, a fair day's work tended to be measured by social wage rather than market forces. The ability of workers to organize themselves into trade unions that collectively bargained for rights, better conditions, and fair pay constituted one of the key elements in the workplace prior to the information age. Through its method of organization, industrial work presented a homogenous experience for workers through standardized work rules intended to promote stability and contractual regulations for entire groups of workers rather than for individuals, which created solidarity in the workplace that could overcome the anonymous aspects of the market.

The developments in the world of work over the last two decades in many Western societies have negated this kind of social contract between the market and the public spheres, as market rules and ideologies were rewritten and the basis of production and industrial relations was radically restructured in a globalising labour market. The worldwide spread of neoliberal capitalism drastically affected Fordist labour market conditions, transforming accepted notions of social responsibility and regulatory work patterns by introducing flexible production methods that have since caused mass redundancies and the deregulation of the labour market and undermined workers' job security. The globalisation of the market dismantled various forms of employment protection and gradually weakened the ability of trade unions to protect their members against a substantial increase in unemployment and dismissal rates.

The deconstruction of employment protection altered the balance of power between capital and labour in a market in which unrestrained international competition occurs. New information and communication technologies have transformed work relations and the industrial relations system to such an extent that workers have begun to feel disenfranchised in a job market in which their rights as participating members have been eroded. Their feelings of insecurity are exacerbated by the Western ideology of individualism, which, in turn, is reinforced by the introduction of individual employment contracts in the workplace. Individual employment contracts have given dismissal powers to employers and added to the vulnerability and insecurity of workers.

My participants all commented, positively and negatively, on the changes in employer–employee relations in the contemporary market. These changes were viewed differently depending on the position of the participant. Both sides of the workforce now view each other with suspicion, and both accuse the other of diminished levels of trust and loyalty. For employers, the central theme of human resource management, or the "excellence" movement it developed into, seeks to guarantee personal involvement and a total commitment to company goals without providing any guarantees of permanent employment. This has resulted in a highly mobile workforce. It is clear from my participants' comments that the social contract of the Fordist era has given way to a work ethic that depends on personal views of, and circumstances in, the labour market, and has given rise to an individual work ethic that is tailored to realizing personal ambitions and requires dexterity in marketing skills.

My study of the consequences for the actors in a globalising labour market has provided evidence to support my argument that a work ethic has different meanings for people with different cultural backgrounds, as it is based on the ideational system and sociocultural environment in which industrial activity takes place. I maintain that work ethic varies in context and essence from culture to culture, and

that workplaces worldwide organise their industrial relations systems according to the influences and dictates of the
culture in which they are embedded. I suggest the notion of
meaning as a process characteristic of the ideational system
of a given society. My findings provided the rationale for my
argument that the changes in the world of work have not affected all actors in the labour market in the same way, as differences in perception of work and expectations of rewards
and goals put them at variance with a work ethic based on
Western ideas about work and life in general. As economic
and political changes followed the rise of technology and
science, the religious aspects of the Western work ethic began to fade, leaving only the expectation of hard work and
economic prosperity.

My study shows that the Maori of New Zealand, who
have been predominantly integrated in the capitalist economy of the country, have different expectations of, and purposes for, their participation in the workforce. My Maori
participants emphasized the importance of Maori working
together in the embrace of their *whanau*, always in consultation with their elders and with an eye on the past and their
recent and distant ancestors. They illustrated this principle
by clarifying that the meetinghouse on the *marae* represents
the founding ancestor within whose embrace the members
of the groups rest. The principle of collective action permeates all Maori economic and social action, in contrast to that
of the Pakehas, who enter the workforce as individuals and
plan for their future independently.

Maori workers who find themselves without a job due to
workplace restructuring or other market constraints appear
to experience less despair than Pakeha workers, as they can
return to the *marae* and be put to work there, or become
streetwise and able to manipulate the system to their own
benefit in order to meet obligations to their *whanau* and
hapu. Losing a job is humiliating to the members of the
whanau and the individual only when such dismissal is the
result of a serious offence or crime.

My participants observed that Maori society had operated perfectly until their institutions were destabilized by the intervention of the Pakeha. Yet Maori have retained many of their customs and institutions. Instead of integrating fully in Pakeha society, they pursued their own avenues toward sociocultural and economic independence.

My research has aimed to show that indigenous people and people from other cultures engage with Western industrial systems in ways that are shaped by their own ideational systems. My study has approached the attitudes of the participants in the world of work by examining their motivations to work and the cultural patterns that give rise to their beliefs about work. Most of all, this has been a study of the *spirit* of work, which cannot be determined by facts or figures, but by the way the people themselves describe their world and their part in it.

References

Applebaum, Herbert A. *The American Work Ethic and the Changing Work Force.* Westport, USA: Greenwood Press, 1998.

Burnett, John, ed. *Useful Toil—Autobiographies of Working People from the 1820s to the 1920s.* London: Allan Lame, 1974.

Crespo, Eduardo, and Amparo Serrano. "The Individualization of Labour, Job Insecurity and Vulnerability and Young People's Experience of Work in Spain." *Transfer, European Review of Labour and Research* 7, no. 2 (2001).

Doing Business in India: A Cultural Perspective. www.stylusinc.com/business/india/business_india.htm, 2010.

Dore, Ronald. *British Factory, Japanese Factory: The Origins of Diversity in Industrial Relations.* Berkeley: University of California Press, 1973.

Dunlop, John T. *Industrial Relations Systems.* New York: Holt, 1958.

Faure, Guy Olivier. "China: New Values in a Changing Society." China Europe International Business School (CEIBS), Academia Sinica Europaea.

Firth, Raymond. *Economics of the New Zealand Maori.* Wellington: A.R. Shearer, government printer, 1972.

Joseph, Fr. Pallath J. "A Study on Doing Business in India: Co-existence of Two Cultures of Conflicting Cultures." Internet document.

Gardner, Katy, and David Lewis. *Anthropology, Developments and the Post-modern Challenge.* London: Pluto Press, 1996.

Gil, David G, and Eva A. Gil, eds. *The Future of Work: A Conference of the Center for Social Change Practice and Theory, 1985.* Cambridge, MA: Scherkman Books, 1987.

Goodenough, Ward H. *Cooperation in Change: An Anthropological Approach in Community Development*. New York: Russel Sage Foundation, 1963.

Gudemand, Stephen. *The Anthropology of Economy*. USA: Blackwell Publishers Inc., 2001.

Handy, Charles. *The Empty Rain Coat: Making Sense of the Future*. London: Arrow Books Ltd., 1995.

Hofstede, Geert. *Culture's Consequences: International Differences in Work-related Values*. London: Sage Publication Ltd, 1980.

Keesing, Roger M. *Anthropology: A Contemporary Perspective*. New York: Holt, Rhinehart & Winston, 1981.

Metge, Alice J. *In and Out of Touch: Whakamaa in Cross Cultural Context*. Wellington, NZ: Victoria University Press, 1986.

Ransome, Paul. *The Work Paradigm: A Theoretical Investigation of Concepts of Work*. Aldershot, England: Ashgate, Hants Publishing Ltd., 1996.

Sahlins, Marshall. *Culture and Practical Reason*. Chicago: University of Chicago Press, 1976.

Sahlins, Marshall, D. *Culture in Practice: Selected Essays*. New York: Zonebooks, 2000.

Salmond, Anne. *Between Worlds: Early Exchange Between Maori and Europeans*. Auckland, NZ: Viking, 1997.

Sinclair, Keith. *A History of New Zealand*. London: Allan Lane, 1980.

Sorenson, John L, "Mormon Worldview and American Culture." *Dialogue* No 8 Vol 2: 17-29, 1973.

Welch, Ruby. *"We Walk Into The Future Backwards": A Case Study of Maori Perceptions of Their Economic Activity*. Unpublished PhD thesis at the University of Queensland, 2007.